www.right-division.com
davereese6@msn.com
Ends of the Earth Mission
PO BOX 4574
Beeville, Texas 78104

MISSION EXPERIENCES AND MINISTRY CHALLENGES
by Dave and Sue Reese

The articles in this book are by Dr. and Mrs. Reese or graduates of Dr. Reese's Bible college, Open Bible College. All are by missionaries with years of field experience.

Dr. Dave Reese attended Memphis Academy of Arts, Samford University, Tennessee Temple University, Temple Baptist Seminary and Trinity Seminary. Graduate work was completed at Temple Baptist Theological Seminary and Trinity Seminary. Dr. Reese started 17 Christian schools in the USA, 3 independent Baptist churches, and pastored Baptist churches for a total of 30 years. He was a faculty member of Tennessee Temple University from 1973-1977 in the Bible department. His last pastorate was Victory Baptist Church Millbrook, Alabama where he served for 17 years until he began foreign mission work in 1993. He is the Founder and President of Ends of the Earth Mission, a mission board dedicated to reaching closed countries and remote regions with the gospel. He and Sue remain active in directing Ends of the Earth Mission.

Mrs. Sue Reese graduated from Open Bible College and completed her RN training at McNeil Memorial Hospital, Chicago, Illinois.

Dave and Sue have been married 64 years in August 2022. They have 5 children, one in Heaven, and 9 grandchildren.

TABLE OF CONTENTS

RETIRING OR REFIRING?

The man turned to face us. One arm was missing. We noticed the man and his wife working on their "oven," a 35-gallon can plastered with mud. Both were retired schoolteachers who entered the mission at 68 years of age. The purpose of the mission training camp is to prepare for survival and a ministry in remote jungle regions. Our fears and complaints faded. If a one-armed, retired schoolteacher can go to the remote jungle to tell others of Jesus Christ, we have no excuse. We must attempt great things for God and expect His power to sustain us.

After pastoring USA churches 30 years, our hearts were stirred for missions. At 55 years of age we had physical difficulties attendant to maturity. Sue needed a hip replacement due to osteonecrosis, a disease that causes bone deterioration. *(From 1993-2022 while continuing in mission work, she had 6 major surgeries for cancer, an internal pacemaker, a Watchman device inserted in a heart chamber, 2 total hip replacements, and one knee replacement. Dave had one knee replacement, back surgery, and a basil artery stenosis.)* Although my health was generally good in 1993, I could no longer "leap over tall buildings with a single bound."

The word of God and world conditions motivated us with comparatively good health to enter foreign mission service; by the grace and mercy of God we continue in spite of aging health problems. 90% of Christian workers labor in only 6% of the world's population. The Lord Jesus Christ said "Go ye into all the world, and preach the gospel to every creature." (Mark 16:18). Surely that statement does not mean the church is to expend the majority of its money and energy within a small circle of the world's population. The apostle Paul's rule of ministry was "to preach the gospel, not where Christ was named." (Romans 15:20). The Church has failed to follow that rule. Over 300,000,000 people have not heard the Name of Jesus in 2020 after 2,000 years of church history.

In our small town there were over 35 churches within a 25-mile radius. Sue and I visited Mainland China and saw many towns and cities with populations of millions and not one gospel witness. Over the jungle terrain of the Amazon in South America, our hearts were stirred again. We wept as the missionary pilot repeated the sad refrain, as we passed over village after village, "As far as we know, this village has never heard the gospel."

Our church was vibrant and growing. We could have settled there for the rest of our life. Looking at the church, I knew those we won and trained over the years could do the job we were doing, and probably do it better. *(Somewhere in my late forties, a good bed began to be more spiritual than a New Year Eve's watchnight service. Fellowships that continued after 9:00 p.m. were no longer my cup of tea.)*

My Assistant Pastor took the pastorate when we left. The church continues to grow. He was a better pastor than I. We did not "lose" a ministry, we simply gained more. The pastor and church are among our dearest friends and supporters.

Physical age and ministry experience is not a hindrance to God's work; it is the cornerstone of it. Older men and women should, by word and *current deeds*, be teachers of the younger. Too many believers think useful work in God's vineyard stopped when Social Security began. We should never retire from God's work. We must constantly refire.

Some allow physical incapacity to hinder their spiritual effectiveness. When my wife and I wrestled with the idea of "crossing Jordan at flood season" there was real concern whether it was faith or foolishness. But as we looked at all the reasons not to step into the edge of the water, we discovered all our fears were either physical or material. There was not one spiritual reason to stay. I can find no Bible verse that excuses us because of age or physical infirmity from the work of world evangelization. Not all can actually go to a foreign field, but there are no excuses for all believers to be active in supporting effective foreign missions.

Sue did have her hip surgery and others. It did not stop our work for the Lord. During the past 30 years, 215 churches were built in the remote jungles of the Philippines. Over 20,000 Filipinos have come to know the Lord. We began our second Bible school in 2004 on the Philippine Island of Mindanao. 5 new churches are planned for every year, pastored by 4 year King James Bible school graduates. We began medical mission clinics and have the facilities to treat Filipinos with free medicine and care.

God allowed us to work during this same period in Communist China and Mongolia. Since 1993 we have been instrumental in placing 35 missionaries in Mongolia, Mainland China and building our own China Christian school with 300 students. Two of our missionaries in China are single ladies over 55 years of age. They love it and are having the time of their lives.

One way we place missionaries in China (closed to normal missionary entrance) is to place them as conversational English teachers. You don't have to be an English teacher to go, but English teaching or any teaching experience is very helpful. A retired person can live and minister in China without difficulty. The Chinese school pays about $600 US per month, provides a furnished apartment, utilities, and in many cases, airfare.

Teaching is a very respected position in China. Age is an asset rather than liability. The oriental culture respects and honors the older person. As you meet people and develop relationships, telling that person of the grace of our Lord Jesus Christ is difficult but once learning the culture is rewarding. Why not consider doing something for God that is exciting, rewarding, and fulfilling?

It is also true that the school of hard knocks is a good teacher. A mature person has the larger portion of essential ministry training complete simply because they have gone through some trouble. Perhaps we must fail in order to be a gracious winner. We must have many dirty valleys to appreciate the clean air of a mountain. We must throw ourselves into useless causes to be more productive in the essential ones. To really know what it means to ride a thoroughbred, we sometimes need to ride all the horses in front of Wal-Mart.

God's calling is not always His enabling. A person in their youth may indeed be "called" to China or elsewhere. But that does not mean they are to buy a ticket without training and preparing. I am sure God did not want me to go to the Philippines the day after I was saved. I needed training and cultural preparation.

For reasons far beyond my small knowledge, God takes a sincere person and turns their "time wasting" into blessings far beyond that anyone could ever anticipate. The resulting ministry is one that is "exceeding abundantly above" all they thought. "For perhaps he therefore departed for a season, that thou shouldest receive him forever." (Philemon 15). This has nothing to do with theological arguments; it has much to do with the provision and wisdom of God, our unhesitating surrender, and the eternal reward of serving Him. –Dave and Sue Reese

A CHRISTIAN KINDERGARTEN IN COMMUNIST CHINA

A young woman was coerced by family members, work mates, and forced by Chinese government law into having her second child aborted. Chinese couples in 1993 were permitted only one child by law under penalty of heavy fines, loss of housing and jobs, and severe public ridicule. This couple already has a sweet little girl. It broke her heart to have this blessing torn from her. Though she knew the Lord through a Canadian female missionary two years before, the pressures of tyranny and her lack of spiritual growth won out in a decision that was hardly just her own to make.

After the ordeal, she began to pray and search for a way she could have more than one child, even many children to hold, love, and help to raise. She decided to take a path of strict personal discipline in order to train herself to train children, and eventually have some kind of school for children.

Not a school operated and controlled by the government, but one that she could call her own. Not a school merely to meet the government's educational agenda, but one where the teachers would genuinely love the pupils as their very own.Sue and I met her on our first trip into Communist China in 1993.

Her name and location are withheld for security reasons. She said to me, "Dr. Reese, would you help me have a kindergarten? Then, I could have all the children for my own!"

She had no money for a building and was already traveling to city areas holding English classes for children in whatever apartment that was available. Her enthusiasm and preparation impressed Sue and me to help. I saw an opening for a missionary training "front" in Mainland China as well. "S" had studied English and skills for teaching English to children. She also studied business to familiarize herself with the education laws in her province.

Eventually she advertised the opening of an English school for children, to be conducted in the evenings. We rented space on the fourth floor of a "cultural palace," something like a community center. Classes were attended by not only kindergarten ages but some parents as well. This was the first English kindergarten in a city of several million population!

We eventually rented our own school building and were able to begin missionary "on the job" training. The school has over 150 students and has provided opportunity for 12 USA missionary teachers to serve as kindergarten English teachers while learning Mandarin language and Chinese culture. We have supported and directed the work there for over 25 years. –Dave and Sue Reese

FIELD EXPERIENCES OF A MISSIONARY IN COMMUNIST CHINA

This missionary is a graduate of my Bible school (Open Bible College) and helped my wife and I with our first introduction trip to China in 1992. "Bob" (name withheld for security of Chinese believers) had worked in Mainland China for 4 years after his graduation from Bible college. He is one of the most knowledgeable authorities on China mission work.

The Lord Jesus Christ has been gracious to allow us to serve Him in China since the beginning of 1990. He has brought across our paths dozens of souls to whom we could personally witness to without fear of being turned in to the authorities. Many of these have found Christ as their personal Saviour. Some have also devoted their life to service to the Saviour. Others are yet timid, and in need of our prayers, uncertain how their profession of faith will affect their survival chances in Communist China.

I hope to encourage those of you who are considering other corners of the field (Matthew 13:38) not to faint in your efforts to arrive where God is directing you, and thrust yourselves into the most important labors taking place in the world....the ministry of reconciliation (2 Corinthians 5:12-21)....the harvest of all who Christ died for, the evangelization of sinners.

Please, Only 15 Minutes a Day

In the front of my English class sat a man in his early twenties who was a "stowaway." He was not a student, but an industrial air conditioning and air quality expert, trained in filtering dust from textile plants.

And does he know textiles! He hoped to listen in to my classes, although he (rightly) figured the college would bar him, once they discovered him there, or they would charge him a prohibitive rate of tuition.

His name is Zhao Xiao-Dong, but we have come to know him as "Samuel." Sam, his wife, Anna, and their little boy, Phillip, just may be the dearest friends we have among the Chinese nationals.

Samuel Zhao followed me back to our apartment that first day we met and asked if he could have only fifteen minutes each day privately with me to practice speaking English. I immediately thought: "If everyone I meet takes fifteen minutes of my day to practice English, I'll be left with no time at all to learn Chinese." Samuel didn't seem like someone too keen on the party system in China, so I decided to take a risk with him. I told him that my primary reason for being in China was not to teach English, and that I really was not interested in attracting private students (I was only obligated to sixteen hours per week in a class environment), but if he was willing to study English from the Bible, I would work with him, and hope that he would also help me with my Chinese.

I was surprised then to learn that an old Christian woman in the city named He Yi-Fang had already been using every opportunity to get the Gospel message to Samuel, and had been praying for God to send a messenger friend to him. Samuel agreed to learn from the Scriptures, and thus God had given me my first Bible student in China.

At first, we would meet out at the soccer field, or on a roadside. He was shy to come to our home. He thought he would be imposing too much to come directly to our apartment, and he was afraid the college officials would cause us trouble if he was found there. But eventually Samuel did begin coming to our home, and our friendship began to run deep.

In time, I began to follow Samuel to his home. Samuel and his wife lived in an apartment consisting of one bedroom, a small entrance area, toilet, and a very small kitchen. All together about 200 square feet. I was made to feel quite welcome, however, and soon humble but delicious meals were being prepared for me at almost every visit.

I was given a gift of a small orange school copy book, full of lined pages, and decided to use it to teach the fundamentals of the Christian faith, beginning with the simple but clear presentation of the Gospel message. At the same time I could study how to present the Gospel clearly in Mandarin Chinese. I would engage Samuel Zhao in this project.

On the left page I wrote simple paragraphs in English, presenting the Gospel of Christ just as if I were dealing with some one who had no knowledge of the Saviour whatsoever: "What Does the Bible Say About God?" "What Does the Bible Say About Jesus Christ?" "What Does the Bible Say About Man?" So on through to the subjects of sin, the Lamb of God, propitiation, resurrection, the Blood of Christ, and so forth.

On the opposite page, Samuel would write out, in both Chinese characters and romanization, a translation in a form of Chinese that the common people could understand readily, including colloquialisms, and useful Chinese idioms that would help to carry the point. Of course to produce an accurate translation required literally hundreds of hours of Bible study with Samuel and discussion about the person and finished work of Christ. Only when I was confident that he understood the subject matter of each section did we settle on the translation.

At the same time, as Samuel explained the finer points of his translating to me, I was being exposed to the Chinese language, and how to use it to get the Gospel to the Chinese people. Getting beyond the subject of salvation itself, we continued the primer with the subjects of water baptism, the church including its offices, the Lord's Table, The Second Coming of Christ, the judgments, Heaven, Hell, knowing the will of God, and others.

Eventually, a second volume was started, dealing with areas such as Finding the Will of God, The Christian Home, Biblical Soul-Winning, How to Study the Bible Effectively, and much more. Needless to say, Samuel was getting a wide exposure to the Words of Almighty God.

As open as Samuel was to the Scriptures, it rather surprised us that he did not get saved sooner than he did. The teachings Samuel had heard about Christ and the Gospel in the past had been confusing to him. The ideas of repentance and what state of mind and heart one must be in in order to be saved were incorrectly conveyed to him by Chinese house church "Christians." So for two years Samuel was under the almost daily teaching of the Word of God before he was saved in 1992.

Samuel taught us how to survive in the modern Chinese culture. Any question we had were answered by him thoughtfully and comprehensively. If we needed something we couldn't find, Samuel would find it and deliver it to our door, or guide us through the city of almost 2 Million people to where it could be found. Whenever something needed repair, it was Samuel who knew just how to handle it. When we needed someone to look after the children, Samuel and Anna were excited to sit with them. When I needed to go to Beijing for anything, Samuel could get the tickets faster than anybody, and would take time off to accompany me if I needed him. If we needed a good doctor for a change, Samuel knew where to find one. In fact, we found the doctor who delivered our son, Abram, through Samuel and Anna. Their child, Phillip, was delivered by the same doctor just a few months before Abram. Simply put, Samuel and Anna are as close as any American friends we have ever had. We love them....and miss them.

Here, in Samuel and Anna, we had met Chinese nationals that were honest and charactered; one hundred percent trustworthy in our book, though they were not yet Christians. We often comment that if professing Christians in America had the character of these two unsaved Chinese, America could evangelize the world in one decade! For two years we kept stressing the urgency of trusting, receiving Jesus Christ.

In April of 1992, the front door of our apartment had been watched daily through binoculars from a window in an adjacent building. We were being watched because of the many visitors to our home who were not associated with the same unit. This made the college officials very nervous, and so surveillance of our apartment was ordered. It may be that there had been an informant in our midst at one time or another. There were a few people who had come in to "spy out our liberty."

Ma Ji, our foreign affairs officer, showed up at our door asking for a list of the names and units of people who were coming to our home. I asked "Jim" how many names would satisfy them and found that five or six names would be enough. It was felt that if they could intimidate just a few people, most others would be afraid to be seen at our home. Therefore, we gave Ma Ji the names of ten people who had visited our home only once or twice and had left business cards (people who wanted something from us for nothing in a material or social sense), had not come for any spiritual purpose, and had no connection with our Bible students. In other words, the People's Public "Security" Bureau would only (or so we thought) be investigating and harassing people who had come to our home basically to pester us, or in some way take advantage of us as foreigners.

Many Chinese have tried to develop relationships with us for what they could get out of us economically, socially, or otherwise. Many Chinese have the chief ambition of getting out of and as far away from China as possible (Can you blame them?), and they need the influence of an American when dealing with the United States Embassy for obtaining visas. They hope we will arrange for sponsors for them in America, and/or recommendations to colleges and universities in the U.S., Canada, England, or Australia. Some even believe that we are so wealthy that we can loan or give them enough money for air fare to the U.S. plus at least one year's tuition in an American university. They are always disappointed with us, because we are just not in the business of helping people leave China for any purpose whatsoever.

Of course, the college officials were well aware of Samuel's frequent visits to our home over a period of two years. Many had seen Samuel and I take off together into town on our Bicycles. Our tightness had become well known. So who was the first person the Chinese secret police hauled in for questioning?

We can't remember now who had informed us that Samuel had been called in for questioning. When we heard, we were shaken, and we began to pray. Samuel was not being held, and our first impulse was to go to his home and learn what was happening. We knew, however, that the police may have also been watching Samuel's home at that point. For many days we had no contact from Samuel at all. I can not describe in words how terrible and helpless I felt, and how fearful I was for Samuel. What had we done?! Had we caused this dear friend to undergo any unnecessary persecution?

Finally, one evening many days later, I could stand it no longer. I grabbed my keys and told my wife that I must go out and find some way to meet with Samuel. I took hold of the latch, pulled the door open, and there Samuel and I stood face-to-face. He had come to our home with the same fears for our family that we had for him and Anna.

Samuel put his hand on my chest and began to push me backward into a room in a far rear corner of our apartment. Once inside the room, he closed the door. We sat and just looked into each others' eyes for a few minutes without speaking. Then Samuel began in hushed tones. "Bob, they've been questioning me about your activities." "How much did you have to tell them," I asked, "and are you in any serious trouble?" Samuel, for my conscience sake, didn't want to give me the details of the interrogation, or how he had fielded their questions. [It is interesting to note here that at times when studying the Gospel accounts (Matthew through John), Samuel often expressed fascination with the skill and cunning used by the Lord when answering the sly questions of the scribes and the Pharisees.] He did strictly warn me to be ever the more careful. Then he gave this testimony:

While I was being questioned I realized that I was actually suffering a degree of persecution for having something to do with Jesus Christ, the Bible, and God's servants. I'm not willing to give up these associations for the sake of government thugs.

But then I thought, "I'm not truly a Christian. Why would I suffer in this life for Christ, and then die and go to Hell?" So when I was sent home, I began to survey afresh all of the Bible teaching of the past two years. I studied many of the verses from the Bible again. There was no further reason to put off receiving Christ.

Bob, I came tonight to tell you that I have trusted Jesus Christ as my personal Savior. I understand the Gospel now. Now it doesn't matter what men may do to me. I am a Christian! God had used this situation to open Samuel's eyes to the truth of the Gospel of the Grace of God.

Samuel has been abundantly blessed by the Lord, not only by saving him, but by putting him in a position where he can more ably serve his Savior. God has promoted him to a position in an import/export company, giving him the opportunity to travel and communicate. Samuel wants to be used as a Bible and tract courier and supplier to missionaries all over northern China. He has already carried hundreds of pounds of material to missionaries around Hebei Province. He needs your prayers for God's protection as he uses his position to further the cause of Christ.

Five young men wanted and needed special attention and direction in the study of God's Word. Several believed the Lord's hand was on them to preach the Gospel and develop ministries to win their own people. We needed a more neutral place to meet, where these men could have a "disconnect" with the others who study the Bible with us, due to the greater degree of risk that may be incurred. It was Benjamin who came forward.

Benjamin Zhao is a mechanical engineer, who at that time was working for a government-run engineering institute. In nine years in that post, he claims to have done only one year's worth of work. This is because there was almost no work to do, and in China, self-initiative is frowned upon.

If the boss doesn't give you a task, sit and do nothing, or invite the wrath of your superior. No supervisor in China wants any self-starter to accomplish something on his own that will put the management to shame. Managers are viciously jealous of any worker who has more on the ball than themselves. Benjamin, being quite a brilliant young man, was naturally frustrated by his situation, so for years had been spending his sitting time (in the office) studying English

When Benjamin was introduced to us, it seemed he was readily predisposed to a study of the Scriptures. He attended our weekly Sunday meetings, and went after the Scriptures with real zeal. After about eight weeks, Benjamin professed Christ as his Savior, and began trying to win his wife to Christ. Before long, he also began to express his burden for the Chinese people and nation. The Lord was dealing with him concerning definite ministry.

Benjamin and his wife had no children. They lived on the fourth floor of a one bedroom flat in a fenced -in compound belonging to the engineering institute. They discussed the risk of hosting a small preachers' class in their apartment. The decided to open their home. Benjamin's wife, to our knowledge, has not been saved, but she saw "a new and fresh thing" in her husband's life, and liked what she saw. She would support his effort to study the Bible.

Every Wednesday evening, as close to sunset as possible (so that there would be few people socializing in and around the compound, and we would be less conspicuous), I and four Chinese men besides Benjamin, would individually enter the compound and find our way through the apartment blocks to find Benjamin's building. We never met in a group outside of the flat, we never all arrived at the same time, nor did we dismiss and leave at the same time. Security is always a concern.

I gave the preacher boys (Benjamin, John, Peter, Joshua, and Mark) reading assignments each week. The assignments were given in such a way as to prompt certain questions and direct them down a certain course in study. The class then began each week with a question and answer session related to the reading assignment. We rarely dismissed before 11 pm, and often we were there as late as 1 am in the morning. For us, this was the first open door to training national workers, so necessary if our ministry is to have any long range effectiveness in China.

One evening at Benjamin's home when beginning our preachers/workers class, as I was opening my Bible to Deuteronomy, John Tie, sitting close on my left, placed his hand on my arm, and asked if he could say something to the class. I gave him place, and he began:

"For many months, I've been studying the Bible with Bob. He and his family have loved me and mine. All of you have prayed for my wife and daughter, who were separated from me by the government when they assigned me to work in this city. I wanted to be like Bob. I wanted my family to be like his family, which we admire. God answered your prayers in re-uniting our family. I have been trying to imitate Bob, even trying to pattern my faith after Bob's. But I have learned that I am not truly saved, and I hope you will help me and pray for me to truly believe on Jesus Christ. John became honest....openly honest. Of course, the Lord is going to do something for people who admit their need, and seek Him (see Hebrews 11:6). I asked the little class to set aside their notes and questions from the assigned reading, and follow along as we go all the way back to the simplicity of the Gospel of the Grace of God.

We started from scratch, as though none of the young men had ever studied the first chapter of the Bible. We reviewed about thirty basic passages on the person and finished work of Christ. We used as many illustrations as the Lord allowed us to bring to mind to simplify our thinking in the matter of personal salvation. We prayed for understanding, and for the Holy Spirit to strip away any blindness in any mind present (see 2 Corinthians 4:3-6). We stressed the full satisfaction that God the Father had in the once-for-ever sacrifice of the Body and Soul of Jesus Christ for the sins of every man (see Colossians 1:20-22; Isaiah 53:1-12)

We left that evening sometime after 11 PM, and John went home still unconverted, but seeking Christ. The following week we had our regular assignment, questions and answers, and took some time to review the Gospel. John said nothing concerning himself, but it was obvious he was still struggling. My family intensified our praying specifically for John. The following wednesday, class began as usual, but John again placed his hand on my arm, and asked to address the class. "Go ahead, John."

"I have something to tell everyone. Last night, while discussing the Gospel with my wife and baby girl, the Lord cleared up my understanding. I trusted Christ as my Savior, and I can tell all of you that I know I am now a Christian. I thank the Lord, and I want to thank all of you for praying for me. I hope the Lord will give me a place to serve Him, and I want to tell others about Jesus Christ."--BP

FOREIGN MISSION WORK IN A CLOSED COUNTRY

It is difficult to explain to folks in the States just how we must operate in a communist country. In America it is taught by some that the following constitutes genuine missionary work:

1. The missionary goes to a foreign country to attend language school.
2. Upon graduation, he rents a roadside building and hangs a sign outside that says "Such and Such Baptist Church" in the native language of his country.
3. The missionary furnishes the building with rows of pews or benches, a piano at front left, organ at front right, and a pulpit at front center.
4. If possible, a baptistry is installed or built somewhere behind the pulpit, or in the floor underneath the choir.
5. Sunday School begins at 9:45 a.m. and "worship" is at 11:00 on a Sunday.
6. The Sunday evening "service" begins at 7:00 p.m. (unless people want to get home early enough to watch TV and say it is to get the school kids in bed early; at which time the service time is 6:00), and there is a "prayer" meeting on Wednesday evening at 7:30.
7. Basically, if the American pattern of "church" isn't copied, it isn't Scriptural, and the missionary should have his support cut off.
8. The missionary hopes that along the way a young man will make a profession of faith and surrender to preach the Gospel (or is that, preach the American model of churchianity).
9. The missionary sends the young man off to another city where his mission board (or a group of agencies which don't get along so well inside the U.S.) has begun an on-field "Bible" institute. After all, like in America, all "calls" to preach are suspect until the "called" has graduated from an *approved* Bible school.

10. After graduating, the national may take over the mission church, so that the American can begin another "work."

We don't argue with much of the above procedure, and we recognize that God has richly blessed the work of many missionaries who have followed that pattern exactly. We praise the Lord for all who have genuinely found Christ in those missions, and for those nationals who have given their lives to full-time Christian service and to winning their own countrymen to Jesus Christ. We add that our purposes also begin in priority with Biblical soul-winning and establishing New Testament indigenous local churches.

We affirm that, regardless of the geography, the Biblical local church is the agency God has established for the unified efforts of believers to carry on the work of Christ in the world, including world evangelism and preparing ministers of the Gospel.

However, if you follow the above pattern exactly and overtly in some countries of the world, (Islamic, Hindu, and communist countries for example), you will be forthwith expelled, imprisoned, or murdered. Your belongings will be confiscated (meaning: stolen). Your converts also could suffer incarceration or death, because you thought only the twentieth century American pattern could possibly be blessed by God.

China and India are the two most populous countries in the world. Together they make up at least one third of the world's population (souls also for who Christ shed His precious Blood and died). Neither China (communist) or India (Hindu and Muslim) currently (1994-2022) allow Westerners to enter as missionaries or evangelists. Then add to these the Islamic countries of Middle East, and other Marxist or Maoist dictatorships on different continents that also ban the open propagation of Christianity.

Then what do we do with "Go ye therefore, and teach all nations,...(Matthew 28:19); "Go ye into all the world,." (Mark 16:15); "Thus it is written, and thus it behoved Christ to suffer, and to rise from the dead the third day: And that repentance and remission of sins should be preached in his name among all nations,..." (Luke 24:46,47) ??!!

In the People's Republic of China, we have used conversational English teaching contracts as a means to legally stay inside the country. We have taught English at colleges and universities for the privilege of living in a land forbidden to men who apply for visas as missionaries. As China has progressed in computer technology, it has become more difficult to enter China as a "foreign expert" unless you have a degree from an accredited state college. (From 1990 to 2000 it was rare for a person to have telephone access — now, it is rare for the average Chinese to be without a cell phone or internet access)

Our purpose is not to be English teachers, but to preach the Gospel and to train men to minister to their own people and plant churches. We use the following method:

1. Enter China officially as a teacher.
2. Study the Chinese language.
3. While fulfilling a contract to teach English for about sixteen hours per week, we develop relationships with our students, their friends, and their families. We also begin to meet many, many other curious Chinese both on and off of the campus.
4. Rarely can we use the college classroom lecterns themselves as Gospel pulpits.
5. We find students who are interested in having a copy of God's word, and we provide Bibles in both Chinese and English (A.V. 1611). As soon as a student expresses any interest in studying the Bible, we schedule times for them, either in our home, or in another safe place.

6. As we worship in our homes on Sundays or other days, we invite students to join us. As we meet nationals from off campus whom we can interest in spiritual things, we invite them also.

7. Every meeting is an evangelistic effort. Many are won to Christ, and begin to develop the Christian graces, and the skills of studying the Word of God.

8. For security purposes, we must limit the number of people who gather in our home at any one time. We must also stagger our schedule to avoid being too conspicuous.

9. Just like missionaries in other countries, we pray and plead with the Lord to specifically deal in the hearts of young men to surrender their lives and skills to continue our ministry to their own people. Several are currently in training.

10. We teach believers the vital nature and responsibilities of local churches. We do not teach believers about church buildings or schedules, pianos or pulpit stands, signs or billboards, pews or carpet, or any other modeling of American churchianity. We teach...THE BIBLE ! We haven't the time for much else. We figure from the warnings in the Acts of the Apostles that the believers will be corrupted soon enough.

11. We don't use a pulpit per se, although some men working in China might. We sit around large tables (by the standards of a Chinese house), where the students can lay out their Chinese Bible and their English Bible (we only give copies of the A.V. in English), song books, notebooks, scratch paper and other articles used in worship and in classroom style study.

12. During our services we occasionally to serve tea or other beverages. At noon and again around 5:30 P.M., meals are prepared for all of us. Students are often studying the Scriptures from midmorning until 9:00 in the evening.

13. While we teach, we allow interruptions for questions, testimonies, and people to get saved (we don't teach them to wait for an "invitation" because in our work the invitation to come to Christ is continuous and perpetual), and to surrender to the Lord for service--BP

THE KING JAMES BIBLE IS TOO HARD FOR ME TO UNDERSTAND

It's amazing to me that Americans claim not to understand the KJB, when a lost Chinaman can get through twenty-seven books twice, and through the Pentateuch once in three months !! I met with a Chinese man every Sunday evening from 7:00 to sometimes 11:00. I answered questions for a while, and then would teach him methods of studying and understanding important Bible themes.

I found my way through a very old cotton mill residential area, and located Hou Yong's apartment. Both Hou and his mother received me with more than common Chinese politeness, knowing that I was a believer in Christ, and had come bearing precious seed. Hou's mother was just about in tears, but it was a joyful flow, believing she was seeing a beginning of her prayers for her son being answered. I spent about one hour in their home that day, just giving Hou some instructions on where to begin reading the Bible. I told him that I would be praying that God would give him the light of the Gospel of Christ. I asked him to read the Gospel of John first, and then he may read from the beginning of the New Testament if he finished John before I returned. And did he read !! That was February, 1991.By May, Hou had read the entire New Testament twice, and had read a large portion of the Old Testament....in a King James Bible !!

Then on one Sunday evening in May, when I entered Hou's home, I noticed something was entirely different. There was an excitement I had never sensed before. Hou's old mama had come into the room with her Bible to study with us. She speaks not a single word of English, and at the time, my Chinese was not far enough along to teach much in Chinese. But something wonderful was in the air. I didn't immediately inquire.

I simply started into our routine."What have you been reading this week, Isaac?" I asked Hou. (I had given Hou the name of Isaac, Son of Promise.) "I've been reading the Book of Hebrews again," was Isaac's answer. "And what in Hebrews has caught your attention so as to draw you into it for the third time?" I wondered out loud. Isaac testified: "I noticed in Hebrews chapter Nine, how that Christ entered into the Holy Place behind the veil with His own Blood. I remember reading about the veil in Matthew, when Jesus died on the cross, how that it was rent from top to bottom. Then I saw that that veil was His flesh. So Christ has removed the barrier."

"And so what does that mean for you in particular?" I eagerly asked. Isaac continued. "Last Tuesday evening, mama and I were discussing these very things, and I realized that God had, by Christ's work, made an access into His presence for every sinner. I am a sinner. And so Tuesday evening I entered by faith in Christ within the veil, into His presence, and have trusted Christ as my own Savior. Now mama and I can both go to Heaven."

God had answered the prayer's of Hou's mama, and her tears were in praise to her wonderful Lord. And I just about shouted all over that cotton mill too. The Bible works anywhere in the world

After these things, Isaac was able to open an English school of his own in that city, and had three classes, totaling about ninety students. Isaac gave Bibles, tracts and study materials to each of his students. From that time, on Sunday evenings, Isaac often had his room full of his students to listen to me preach the Gospel to them. What a joy to see the Lord work. God saved some of those students. And several times I found myself at Isaac's English school teaching the Bible, and preaching the Gospel. I was discovering that God's hand is not shortened, even inside of a communist country.--BP

COLLEGE EDUCATION IN COMMUNIST CHINA

Every high school senior in China takes a college entrance examination. The passing score for entrance to the basic institution of higher learning is a 60 (points). In fact, this is the score necessary for passing any and every exam a student ever takes, and tests are deliberately designed to fail ten percent of the class. But fewer than ten percent of Chinese high school graduates ever get to college. Depending on your score above 60, and determined by what specialties the national government thinks it needs in society, students will be assigned to China's wide ranging assortment of institutes, colleges, and universities.

It is important to remember, especially if you are working daily with college students, that students do not choose their college or major. This is unless the family of the student is wealthy or politically powerful, and can afford to pay the tuition themselves, instead of relying on the government, which ninety-nine and nine tenths percent must. This is because all people in socialist countries are equal, *of course*.

While in the city of Shijiazhuang, Central China (1990-1992), I lived and taught at a geology college. Upon a survey of my forty undergraduate students, I found that only one young man, named Zeng, "liked" his major. This young man, age twenty-two, came to ask for my eleven year-old daughter's hand in marriage once, and within two weeks of my pre-1940's style fatherly... well, let's just say "reply," Zeng attempted suicide from a fourth story window. You may draw your own conclusions. Most geology students have the fear of being sent to coal mines upon graduation, or to the Gobi Desert to hunt for minerals.

In 1993 and 1994, I taught at an Agricultural University in Northeast China. My survey of students revealed a slightly higher positive response to the college and to their individual majors, but then this is the same group that "volunteers" to manually clear ice and snow from public roads, for no compensation, "for our country". Most of the students at the Agriculture University are from this particular province, which is considerably more politically conservative than Central and South China.

Whereas in the United States "conservative" refers to the moderate to right wing of the Republican Party, plus a few "Reagan Democrats" and independents, the word "conservative" in China means those who are hanging on to Chairman Mao Ze-Dong's failed teachings.

In the "Peoples'" Republic, geology, agriculture, and like colleges are considered to be at the lower end of the spectrum with regard to the respect they command from the general public and academia at large. And teachers' colleges fare no better! There are some institutions though that are respected: Beijing University, Qinghua University, and Zhongshan University, to name three which are pretty well known. That is, at least in Asia, and many developing countries around the world. Beijing Languages Institute is one of the best language training schools in the world for about six major world tongues. I have only been considered for contracts by colleges at the lower end, because my own major and background are not in English education.

So students arrive at college at eighteen years of age or a little older (my freshmen at Northeast Agricultural University averaged twenty years old), and of course, like young freshmen in any country, begin new experiences that excite them, within the context of China's limited social strata.

They make new friends, begin a socially and politically suppressed interest in the opposite sex, learn new study habits, begin to miss their families and home towns, get interested in the local fashions and entertainments, and learn new living restrictions.

Students are introduced to the three to five other roommates with whom they will share one eight foot by ten foot cubicle in a concrete dormitory block; the walls, unsealed, and hold only chalky whitewash. Four such cubicles will share one wash area, where human bodies, clothing, and eating utensils will all be hand-scrubbed, almost always with cold water.

This area also houses the "squat-pot" toilets; sometimes partitioned off, and sometimes not. Students may carry glass thermos type bottles to central boiling plants once or twice daily (I just learned they must pay two "fen," or .80 of a cent per thermos), if they desire hot water for sponge bathing, cleaning, or tea drinking.

On certain assigned days, students may carry their towels, soap dishes, and shampoo bottles to central bath houses, like we used to do when camping in California's state parks (These bath houses are not as clean as those in the state parks.). Such shower rooms are divided male from female, but there are no individual stalls for privacy, like Army basic training. Most Chinese do feel ashamed of their naked bodies, and this situation is left as is to further enforce society's commonality.

One to two yuan (eleven to twenty-two cents) per day is paid to eat at centralized dining facilities, literally, "mess halls." College meals are never like Mother's home cooking, but they ought to be more than "enough to keep body and soul together," which is precisely the way students here describe them.

And I have eaten with the students, so I am aware of the diet on which they must make their brains function, day in and day out. One Sunday evening, one of my premier students came around the house warning us about the problem of hepatitis being contracted in the dining hall.

Chinese claim they don't eat as much meat as Americans. They don't eat meat fillets like Americans, but they probably eat as much meat overall, and five times as much animal fat. Tendon and muscle are too expensive, about one U.S. dollar per pound. College students' intake of meat is tightly restricted, however.

Once I asked a class, "Do you know the meaning of 'microscope'?" One of my better students in love with comedy answered, "A microscope is the device we must use if we want to find the meat in our rations at the dining hall." And then, the diet also differs according to a family's financial capability to send extra allowances to their student child, so that he or she can go out for a restaurant meal once in a while, or buy junk food, Chinese style, which is abundant.

Students are aroused each morning, except Sundays, by loudspeakers playing revolutionary music, "stirring" spoken messages, or other announcements from their fearless leaders. First, they sponge bathe and brush their teeth. Then, they exercise, and work up a sweat. The idea of exercising and then bathing before breakfast and class somehow doesn't occur to them. Up at five thirty, breakfast at six thirty, and then to the classroom for reviewing lessons before the class day begins at eight o'clock. Some listen to the radio before class. English lovers often try to tune in to Voice of America or British Broadcasting Corporation to work on their listening comprehension. Russian language students have no problem finding programs out of many cities North of the border.

The average class day is six hours long, including breaks. Actual lecture time though, doesn't generally go beyond four and one-half hours at the agriculture university where I taught, but five and one-quarter hours at the geology college. The students are most often bored to tears with their teachers, who still use very traditional methods of instruction: standing poker faced front and center, speaking with monotone voices. And remember: most students are not interested in the course when they enter the classroom. When asked a question, students stand up at attention like a buck private and try to answer. When they want to ask a question, they sit up straight, fold the arm tightly at the elbow, and tight up against the body, putting the palm of the hand toward the face, the tips of the fingers never higher than than one's own head. Class Instruction is a very rigid procedure.

The classroom buildings are also mammoth concrete boxes, with almost no architectural flair whatsoever, unless built prior to 1949. The concrete is not sealed, so they don't dare use any kind of paint that restricts moisture, as it will peel off in no time, and the plaster surfaces will erode. A white chalky "paint" is used, which comes off on your clothing exactly like chalk from the blackboard. There is no floor covering, which is probably wise. In the Springtime, when all the snow and ice begins to thaw on the roof, water seeps through, and down the walls for three or four floors, and washes the whitewash off, leaving the walls bare, and the floor covered with large white puddles.

The very simple desks and podiums are made from wood stained brown, or from painted sheet metal. Chairs may be somewhat modern in design, or may be slatted wood, like home made Sunday School benches. They are almost always filthy dirty, or covered with chalk dust.

Sometimes chalk board erasers are pounded out on the desks, and the next user of the room must clean up the mess. Desks are etched by pocket knives with Chinese calligraphy and English words. The insides of the desks are full of waste paper and cigarette butts. Even the teacher's podium (I never use it), always requires cleaning prior to class.

Classroom walls are filthy with hand prints and foot prints! The windows are opaque with cigarette smoke, air pollution and dust. The fluorescent light fixtures have three-eighths of an inch of dirt on them. Smoking is not allowed in the classrooms during class, but it is permitted in the corridors, and in classrooms at other than class times. Students are allowed to use the rooms for parties, at which sunflower seed hulls, watermelon rinds cigarette butts and ashes, and trash just go on the floor. They sweep it out afterwards, but they never really get it clean. Often there is a party's stench left over for Monday morning's class.

Hold your nose while at the ends of the corridors, where the restrooms are located. And what a joy to have a classroom near the restrooms! The smell of urine would knock a buzzard off a dung wagon. This is, of course, more severe in the summer when warmer air circulates through the corridors.

Students take a lunch break from eleven thirty to one thirty each midday, then return to the classrooms, laboratories, or wherever, for a couple more hours of learning. And there are included physical education classes and team sports. Then the remainder of the afternoon is free for other activities.

Between three thirty and five thirty each afternoon of pleasant weather, the basketball, volleyball, badminton, and tennis courts fill up with students. When the ground dries out enough, the soccer football fields will also be well occupied.

Most of the girls, however, take long walks or jog, with only a few participating in any sports on a court. No sports requiring very much equipment are played, simply because neither the colleges or the students have the money to spend on such gear. So, although there is a curiosity about baseball, American or Canadian football, and hockey, these sports are never seen on college campuses. More students than ever are gaining an interest in tennis, however, finding the money to spend on a racquet and some balls is a problem.

At about five thirty in the evening, the mess hall is open, and the students dig deep for a few more pennies. Afterward, it's back to the classrooms, large lecture halls, and the library for a couple of hours of study and review of the day's lessons. The students have their favorite spots to which they head, expecting to find buddies or girlfriends with which to "study." There are a few regular and remedial classes held in the evenings, especially in the foreign languages and computer sciences: classes that tend to generate more interest because the students feel these classes may help their future. Becoming a translator or banging on computers for foreign owned enterprises are much-sought-after goals. And of course, these disciplines will help graduates get an opportunity to "study abroad," which in most cases really means "Get out of China by any (honest or deceptive) means possible."

I previously mentioned that students have a suppressed interest in the opposite sex. I am, however, surprised to see this less suppressed in northeast China than in central China. After a couple of hours of self-study in the evenings, it is common at the agricultural university now to see dozens of couples strolling arm-in-arm, after dark, looking for places to be alone. And if one has to be out in the evening hours, it will be discovered that the basketball and tennis courts become a place for a different kind of sport, some of which is not very discreet. Why are the bushes shaking? The reasons for this are not difficult to figure out.

This author was married at the age of twenty, and his wife gave him their first child before he was twenty two. Chinese young men are forbidden marriage licenses until age twenty five. Young women must be twenty three. And the government rewards late starters, say, twenty eight to thirty year olds. These, along with forced abortion and abortion on demand, are population control policies. I have graduate students who are single in their early thirties, and claim they don't even have girlfriends or boyfriends!!

Someone is pulling our leg just a bit, don't you think? I mean, let's be real. For starters, Chinese students have Darwin's evolutionary theory drilled into them from childhood. Religious influences, except demonic mysticism (the martial arts, and so forth), are discouraged, especially Christianity. There is no sound spiritual training, and hence no substantial moral foundation. Also, China has been importing the music of the sex and drug sub-cultures of the United States and Europe since 1980. Michael Jackson is one of the very favorite recording artists among the younger set. Western fashion, including the attire of harlots (quite literally), is coveted by almost all young women in the cities. And we are expected to believe that the overwhelming majority of Chinese young people, forbidden marriage until their mid-twenties, are never involved in sexual promiscuity. If you believe that, I have a toll bridge across the Grand Canyon I'd like to sell you...cheap, too.

Toward the end of May, 1994, the Agriculture University had its annual Spring sports meet. I was asked to participate, and at first agreed, even though totally disinterested (I like baseball. Later, I decided it would really be ridiculous and childish for me to throw the shot put, just to entertain a crowd, so I withdrew. The University put my name on the event roster anyway, believing the students would see it and coerce me into participating.

You see, I know from the few intellectually honest students that any student who doesn't participate in an event will receive punishment of one kind or another. This goes for teachers also. Since they are coerced, they don't mind trying to coerce me, too.

Okay, you may think I have crossed the threshold into pure cynicism. Only westerners who have lived here...long enough, can understand what I am saying. To illustrate: Our Chinese friend and brother, Matthias, and I went into the university's mail room when nobody else was there. I checked my box, but he had no key to the box that belongs to his department.

Matthias explained that all of his classmates receive their mail through the same box, and only one student holds the key. A special kowtowing relationship must be established with that "key" student, if you want your mail on time and without a department-wide search. And of course, often THE MAN WITH THE KEY IS NOT HERE, so you'll just have to wait for that letter of comfort and encouragement from home. This is a way for one student to exert any power he can over others, since the opportunities to advance in meaningful ways in this society are rare. An adult student with the right to the key can bully other students to satisfy his craving for position.

Even teachers don't have keys to their own classrooms. A student monitor has the key. I, along with two dozen students, on occasion have been denied entry for class, just because "THE MAN WITH THE KEY WAS NOT HERE." I, a teacher, have asked for keys to my own classroom(s), and have always had my request ignored.

At the end of three, four, or more years of political conditioning called a college education, students can allow the college or university to assign them to work units all around China which come bidding for graduates. This used to be the strict rule of the matter, but alas, things are changing, even if only for the immediate expediency of the Chinese communist regime.

Students can find jobs on their own, or strike out on their own as entrepreneurs. In any case, somebody will find be responsible to pay off the college for the education. Any company hiring a graduate will pay a certain sum of money to the college. If the graduate goes it alone, then some deal must be struck. --BP

THE INTERNATIONAL DEBT

"Withhold not good from them to whom it is due, when it is in the power of thine hand to do *it*." Proverbs 3:27
"I am debtor both to the Greeks, and to the Barbarians; both to the wise, and to the unwise." Romans 1:14
"So, as much as in me is, I am ready to preach the gospel to you that are at Rome also." Romans 1:15

We hear a lot about the national debt and balancing the budget. However, it is much talk and very little action. There is another debt, greater by far, serious, and more damaging than any monetary debt.

It is a debt owed by every saved person to every person to whom the gospel has not been preached. The debt is to tell these who have never heard about Jesus. It is not discharged in local work. It is not relieved after a few years of faithful work. It is not removed after multitudes have been saved through our personal work. There is no discharge of the debt on this side of glory. It is continuing and growing each day. This debt has been growing for almost 2,000 years!

Paul said, **"So, as much as in me is..."** Is that our case? I'm afraid not. The Church has not given its whole being to this great work. When we "sell out," only then will we begin to discharge the debt. Too many churches and Christians have decided to do more for missions *after* the nursery wall is painted and *after* the new car is paid off. When Jesus returns, we will regret this selfish misdirection.

We delight in examining each other's religious credentials. We glory in comparing our attendance records. We are desirous to learn new prophecy guesswork while millions die and go to a Christless eternity.. How will all this look at the judgment seat of Christ?

Our debt is not to learn more prophecy, perfect our Christian walk, or increase Easter Sunday attendance. Our debt is to tell those who haven't heard of Jesus and His saving grace. The result of prophecy or Bible study should impel us into all the world with the gospel. Too often the sad result "Christian growth" is the founding of a new Bible study or church on a street already dotted with churches. –Dave Reese

EXPERIENCE

Experience? When reading this you may think this mission director is a braggart. After dealing with Chinese for 30 years on all levels from national leaders to village commoners, I still feel as though I know very little. China is a difficult culture to understand.

One of the frustrating things about founding and directing a foreign mission work is when an American missionary goes to a strange culture like China and finds it really *is different from his USA life,* he or she, after a month or so, begins to think since we don't live in the same city as they, we really don't understand what the problems are.

Some become experts in all phases of the work. Then the emails, letters, phone calls begin to pour in back home with the "poor me" attitude or the Lone Ranger complex. The ones who do survive are those who realize they don't know anything, content themselves with being a student of the culture, slow down and trust the Lord, and trust the church and mission leadership that got them on the foreign field.

If a total was made of the trips and stays in China, we lived there 3 years. We have traveled on bicycles, motorcycles, trains, farm crop tractors, buses, taxis, subways, private cars, horses, cadaboa, and airplanes over many miles in many places. We walked for miles through countrysides where no American or foreigner walked in seventy-five years.

In Mainland China we've stayed in Beijing, Harbin, Guangzhou, Shenzhen, Chengdu, Chongqing, Kunming, Taiyuan, Guiyang, Shenyang, Haikou, Wencheng, Sanya, and a score of other smaller villages, towns, and teeming cities. With extensive travel through the Provinces of Heilongjiang, Jilin, Liaoning, Hebei, Shanxi, Henan, Hubei, Hunan Jiangxi, Guangdong, Guizhou, Sichuan, Yunnan, and Hainan provided first-hand knowledge of China that hundreds of millions of even Chinese will never have and much more than some foreigners who have lived there in one spot for years. What is a law in one Province may not be in another and most locals simply will not travel out of their area to learn that fact.

We have had our share of diarrhea, fever, broken teeth and other physical discomforts. Chinese medicine is no stranger. Tiger urine and ox bone marrow works. We know what a WC is and everything we wish we did not know about them. We have eaten rice in many forms, fish, chicken cooked, as well as pieces with blood still dripping, donkey, ducks, tea-eggs, other eggs, pork, pure fat, cabbage, steamed bread, potatoes fried, roasted (even sweet potatoes baked in a fifty-five gallon can on the street) moon cakes, cookies, dog, frog, eel, snake, crab, prawns, worms, cornshuck soup with fish bladders, and a hundred other things un-named. We have imbibbed enough tea of all kinds to float a battleship.

From fancy restaurants with the Provincial leaders (Mayors, University Presidents, Education Department Heads, Foreign Affairs Officers, Business people) to local cadres and nationals in street cafes, to students in school cafeterias, to many homes, we understand eating in China.

Our stays in English teachers' apartments, Chinese homes, cheap Chinese hotels with water on the floor, rats, roaches, and bedbugs, as well as the Five Star hotels has helped us know what it is to take no showers for several days, G-I showers, and what it means when it is 0 degrees and there is no hot water. We understand dung on the streets and the stench of raw sewage where you are trying to eat. We've seen the abandoned babies on the street and the cripples pulling themselves along. The many faces strained by years of oppression burn in our memories. The frustration of nothing working like we think it should work is a repeated experience of many years. Promises (in my thinking) have been broken so often, it is expected.

Meetings and conferences are many. We meet with the top officials of Education and Foreign Affairs in Beijing. We meet with Foreign Affairs Officers of several provinces. We talk with school principals, Chinese teachers, and English teachers. We endured hours of business schemes by factory managers and looked at plans of individuals for mechanized maniquins, bicycles, fish oil, and dried food. All necessary to place missionaries as English teachers in order to get the gospel into a closed country.

We listen for hours to Chinese students as they tell their plans and dreams; answer their questions and converse with them. We have been in many secretive meetings with students to teach them the Bible. We whispered and turned the radio or TV on to disquise our conversations in hotels. We have talked with Chinese Christians who spent years in prison for their faith and others who suffer many hardships for the Name of Jesus Christ. We understand something of Christianity in China. We visited the Three Self churches and know somewhat of its problems.

Language problems are many. It is unfortunate that our work takes us to countries with different languages like Mongolia, Mexico, Philippines, China and several other places. We do not have the luxury of settling down in one place and learning one language. We are like kindergarten students in Spanish, Ilonggo, Cebuano, Tagalog, Mongolian, Cantonese and Mandarin. We confuse "Como usta usted" with "kamusta" and "Como se yama" with "Sino nalen mo" in Spanish and Ilonggo. We get tones all confused in Chinese and pronunciation all mixed. Perpetual students of several languages, we know the importance and frustrations of language study.

Reference books on China by those who lived there fill our bookcase. We absorb every cultural item we can. But we learn most culture from the horse's mouth. Every situation and meeting is a classroom for me. I look at who talks and where people are seated. I observe who enters the room and when. My questions to a Chinese while riding through the city are not items of idle curiosity, but information to help me understand this strange land.

We listen to school leaders tell us what is wrong with a teacher; we listen to teachers telling us what is wrong with the school. We see plans succeed and fail. Three critical times our whole mission work in China almost collapsed because missionaries did not do the right thing. We worked through all of them.

We have placed seventeen people in China in various areas over the past 9 years. We have visited with all of them and know the places, demands, and what they face.

In addition to China, we have slept in the steaming jungles of the Amazon, traveled the streams with naked savages, spent many nights in nipa huts in the Philippines' and had injuries from a motorcycle wreck fifty miles from nowhere in the Mindanao mountains, along with several life threatening situations with NPA guerillas and Muslim extremists, slept in gers and rode in a Russian jeep for hundreds of miles in Mongolia, walked where Paul walked in Galatia, made unending drives in Canada, preached on the street in New Zealand, ate goat soup in rancheros in the mountains of Mexico, broke a tooth on hard bread in Northern Ireland, and spent the night in every state in the USA.

If you boil the problems down to major categories, problems in Mexico, China, the Philippines, or the USA—all are the same:
Food
Transportation
Living Quarters
Clothing
Job
Other People
Health

Most Americans don't know what real hardship is in these areas. We are rich and do not know it. When the silver spoon is pulled out of our mouth, and life as it has been lived for generations by millions around the world falls, we expect the Purple Heart.

Do we have experience? Yes, and most of it in the University of hard knocks. Know anything? Not very much. We continue to be students.—Dave Reese

BIBLICAL CRITICISM

In the original languages (notice the term *languages*) of the Old Testament text, the Massoretic text is the preserved word of God. In the New Testament text, the Received or Majority text, is God's preserved word. We do not accept the higher criticism theories of "better manuscripts" being discovered during the 1800's. Therefore, we do not believe translations that base their text on anything other than the Massoretic and Received text are reliable. Modern versions do contain much of the word of God but have certain text errors and attack the Deity of Christ and the blood atonement. The majority of modern Biblical criticism has produced nothing but confusion among churches and believers.
Those who translate from the Hebrew and Greek texts should do so with utmost reverence and caution. There is a great need for the word of God to be translated into languages where it does not exist but that translation work should be done by those who not only have expertise in the source and target languages, but who also know manuscript evidence and Church history.

BALANCE and COMMON SENSE

While taking a strong stand on the Bible issue, we realize there are those who differ. We attempt to avoid needless arguments or bring reproach upon the Name of Christ by getting sidetracked or unbalanced as to the real world in which we live.

For example: What does the Bible issue matter to the man who lives next door to a King James Bible church if no one tells him about the Lord and he dies and goes to hell? What does it matter if we take a strong stand on the Bible, and argue with the brethren over the issue, but make no effort to get that Bible translated into the 3,000 tongues without one verse in their language?

How will it go at the Judgment Seat of Christ for that NIV missionary who dedicated his life to carry the word of God to a tribe without a Bible verse? How will it go for the KJB only pastor who threw scraps to world missions while he spent thousands writing books to attack the NIV? If you had to choose a pair of shoes, which one would you pick?

All of the "Bible-believing" brethren should be weeping over the lack of the word of God in 3,000 languages rather than majoring on fighting others who differ with them. All the modern translators should be on their knees, begging God to forgive them for the millions of dollars spent on repetitious and superfluous scholarship while over 300 million souls have not heard the Name of Jesus one time in their life. In light of the great worldwide need for the word of God in every language, there is absolutely no justification in the attempts to replace the King James Bible among English speaking peoples.

TRANSLATION

It is our duty to translate the word of God into languages that do not have a reliable translation. Translation work should be a team effort by those who are thoroughly versed in the history and content of English Bible translation, the Received text, textual criticism (including the critical apparatus of Nestle's Greek text) and manuscript history.

Only those who are doctrinally sound should do translation work. Further qualifications require ability to fluently speak and write in the target language. There is no such thing as a "word for word" translation from one language to another, so it is evident a variety of sources would be necessary to accurately transmit the word of God. For example: In a language where there is no concept of "believe" how would one translate "Believe on the Lord Jesus Christ"? Other terms such as justification, regeneration, etc., carry a great load of responsibility when we think about accurately conveying what those terms mean in a Bible context and how the locals will understand our effort.

A translation should also be tested by various practical means to investigate its spiritual fruitfulness and how it speaks to the local in his heart language.

Where an accepted translation already exists on the foreign field or at home, and is trusted by believers, all diligence should be given to not cast doubt on the integrity of the translation. Many novices, eager to translate, solve one problem but introduce ten new ones. It is far better to work out perceived translation errors using the accepted text rather than throwing it out altogether. In this area, modern English translations failed. Careless scholarship, fueled by the fire of publishing houses making money, has made Bible translation a business rather than a ministry. The end result has been to make many question the word of God rather than induce careful and reverent study of it.

MONEY AND THE MINISTRY

Here is what you are about to read:

1. First of all, define and justify the main goal.
2. The ability to make quick, on the spot decisions without waiting to have a committee or deacon meeting, is a priority issue when you are dealing with urgent matters.
3. There are no quick fixes, no magic formulas, and no guarantees at any time.
4. Convince and lead a small number of serious and responsible individuals and you will have no trouble with larger numbers.
5. When problems arise, the best course to take is to listen to your critics and if they are right, change.
6. Learn to listen to experienced and successful members in your church.
7. When it is evident something doesn't work, drop it, but make sure it is not your impatience that makes you change.
8. Exercise your spirituality in a closet but roll your sleeves up and get to work on the street.
9. Money alone should not be the major factor in any work, secular or religious.
10. A great marriage is the best thing under the sun; it will get you through thick and thin.
11. If you don't really like where you are or what you are doing, you can not succeed.
12. Keep your eye on the major goal; focus stirs enthusiasm.
13. Hesitancy is a killer.
14. When you are ready to quit, remember anybody can run from a problem.
15. Forget your failures but evaluate your mistakes and determine to not repeat them.
16. Be a compassionate dictator.
17. Concentrate on developing confidence and inspiring people.
18. Break up the big goal into smaller, attainable ones.
19. Have a positive message in all classes and services.
20. Put life into the regular scheme of services.

21. Bring quality preachers into the pulpit for special meetings.
22. Get the right man to do the job and it will be done right.
23. Simplify the budget into broad categories and cut the nonessentials.
24. Above all, get involved in people's lives outside the pulpit.
25. Get together with the key *men* of the church and new prospects, outside the pulpit, at every opportunity.
26. You need a time when you systematically teach the Bible outside regular pulpit hours. Pastors commit a major error in neglecting this avenue or turning it over to others.
27. Do not waste your time on visitation that does not produce fruit.
28. The most ineffective thing you can do is to try the job *all by yourself*; the second most ineffective thing is to *let others do it all*.
29. Give the church a jolt in the arm at least once a year.
30. Disband all committees.
31. Organization should be based on as simple a structure as possible.
32. Church staff members should be added only after they prove themselves as church members.
33. Train a "Timothy" to take your place.

"For the love of money is the root of all evil: which while some coveted after, they have erred from the faith, and pierced themselves through with many sorrows." (1 Timothy 6:10).

A church can not be built without money but every church that is built right will have adequate funds to do its ministry and do it with an honest conscience. There are dishonest ways to gather money but God does not bless those who practice the love of money. All crooks are not in the Casinos, some deal the cards from a church pulpit.

Many try to *get money* so they can build a church or increase its ministry.

This is getting the cart before the horse. Building a church means interaction with *people*, winning them to Christ and building *people*. God never promises to bless money-gathering efforts; He does promise to bless proper church (people) building. Go after *people* for the right reason and the money will come in due season and in the proper proportion.

As I tell you the little I know about money, we need a background. I'd like to give you a personal *case study*. It's real. I lived it.

Having the dubious distinction of being sued by another pastor involving courtroom, lawyer, jury, and all, money is an interesting subject for me. Forty-five years ago a church $350,000 in debt called me as pastor. Reduced to thirty-five members by several inept pastors, the last being the worst, the church was a mess.

It took us one year to straighten most of the financial mess out. Immediately, the former pastor sued the church for money. The irony of the thing is that the first message he preached at the church was the text above; the last thing the church heard from him was a lawsuit over money. After the lawsuit he began to perm his hair, wear makeup and paint his nails. Now he is dead.

We moved there-all eight members in my household. Neither the lawsuit nor the debt stopped us. Over the period of seventeen years I pastored the church, membership increased, bills were paid, buildings were built, future leaders trained, and an excellent reputation developed. The man I trained has been the pastor for the past nine years and the church continues to grow. He is a better pastor than I ever was.

Nine years ago my wife and I left that church to enter mission work. We started "all over" again: no money and no promises, and fifty-five years of age. From 1993-2004 we started twenty-eight churches in the Philippines, trained over fifty Filipinos who are in the ministry, placed thirty missionaries in other fields, started a mission board, and in 2001 received through the mission over $600,000 which went directly out to missionaries in five countries. *(At present – 2022 – Philippine churches started are over 200; Resident Bible schools are 2 plus 4 satellite internet classes; trained Filipinos are over 250, and missionaries are 47)*

Why did we take a church in debt? Why did we leave it after things were going well? Why didn't we join an established mission board instead of going it alone? These are decisions that make only little sense (to certain people) at the time. Most folks think you have a ministry death wish. All of it has to do with the will of God.

The will of God is not some mysterious, ethereal experience. God is more practical than we are and has much more common sense. I've never had a vision or seen an angel. If I did, I'd run, or get me a 900 number and go on TV. Perhaps in both cases, church and mission, the only "spiritual" thing I can identify was a sense of calm that all was OK. We did pray and ask God to keep us from ourselves but I've learned not to trust *my* prayers too much. After all, "we know not what to pray for as we ought." (Romans 8:26).

On the practical side, I can point to several reasons.
1. I knew most of the people at the troubled church from a previous pastorate. They are quality people and needed help.
2. At the time they requested us to come I was teaching at a Bible College started by a local Baptist church and in the 1970s was the largest church in the world. Some newly

hired professors were moving the school away from the King James Bible towards any new translation that came down the road. I was too much of a Bible believer for most of them and conflicts developed. My classes were full; the majority of their students were "drafted." Envy and nit picking became frequent and I saw where the school was heading. We decided to go where folks needed and wanted the Book.*(At present – 2022 – the church and school is no longer in existence. They forsook the KJB and paid the price of apostasy)*

3. I've always enjoyed a challenge. It is exciting to stand back and watch the Lord part your Red Sea, put you through on dry ground, and drown your enemies.

The practical reasons for leaving the church I built and going into missions?

1. We were too comfortable. I could have coasted and rocked on the front porch of our new home. We didn't have to pray anymore about thin tires on the car or where our next meal was coming from.
2. We are convinced that more and more churches in the USA are farming the high places and doing less and less while the majority of the world goes to Hell.
3. We trained sufficient leadership in our church so that a duplication of leadership existed.
4. I knew a little about pastors, their problems, responsibilities, and how they think.
5. We thought about the Red Sea and the River Jordan again.

We do not write these things as experts. Really, I know nothing. I still feel like a novice in church matters. It is like walking on eggs. There are no quick fixes, no magic formulas, and no guarantees at any time. Unless God gets into our lives along the way, all is vanity. When we begin to think God is using us, He is gone. I suppose Paul had this in mind when he spoke of working "out your own salvation with fear and trembling." (Philippians 2:12).

A church of 30-100 members is a good proving ground on money matters for a pastor. Convince and lead a small number of serious and responsible individuals and you will have no trouble with larger numbers. The principles remain the same. This is not to say that tribulations are absent. Situations arise that try your very soul and make you write a resignation letter for each one.

When problems arise, the best course to take is to listen to your critics and if they are right, change. Learn to listen to experienced and successful members in your church. Even if they are not right, it might be good to try it out. If we get too old to learn, brick walls break heads. Without good members in that "broke" church, we never would have turned it around.

Flexibility is also indispensable. When it is evident something doesn't work, drop it. Make sure it is not your impatience that makes you change. God did not give you a special dispensation of knowledge when you stuck that "Reverend" on your name. Just remember that a pulpit and common sense rarely meet each other.

Stickability. Staying with the task is usually a lesson learned too late. When you are ready to quit, remember anybody can run from a problem.

One more day or week can turn things around. Besides, *if you are doing what God wants done in the way He wants it,* all His enabling is at your hand or else He is not God. If He can't straighten out that little problem, you might as well start flipping hamburgers or selling cars.

It could be your goal is right but your method is wrong. It is also possible that your calendar and God's are not in synch. God uses wait time to correct and instruct.

Hesitancy is another killer. Why walk around a chair for thirty minutes? For the love of Pete, move it or sit down! I've seen so many Christians "praying" about petty decisions for months and never getting anything done, it is enough to make you puke. Exercise your spirituality in a closet but roll your sleeves up and get to work on the street. Nobody really cares how long you pray about sitting down; God doesn't either. When the room is dark, don't pray for someone to turn on the switch. *Mash it.*

Money alone should not be the major factor in any work, secular or religious. In the move from Bible school to the church, the financial picture looked bleak. I made $350 a month as a Bible teacher. We had started a church while teaching and the church paid for our house and utilities. I also started several Christian schools during that time that paid the food bill for my wife and me, our five children, and two aged aunts. Taking the broke church meant a cut in pay, stepping into a financial morass, as well as a possible ministerial disaster.

Before I was saved, the majority of decisions were made on the factor of money involved. In 1963 I trusted Christ and left that life. We moved to Birmingham, Alabama and began college without a cent.

At that time Sue and I had two children and a Siamese cat. The only thing we lost in the move was the cat. By the grace of God and a good wife, I graduated from seminary in 1970. Did we have to work? Are you kidding?? I worked on vending machines for a while and then for the last six years of school worked second shift in a machine shop. Sue worked in hospitals until babies made it clear to us a Mom at home is more important than money in the bank. (This means I am not patient with anyone who says they didn't go to college because of money).

A great marriage is the best thing under the sun. It will get you through thick and thin. When I quit, Sue was there to make me go again. When Sue quit, I somehow believed it would work out. By the way, marriages based on money are doomed to failure. Sue and I lived in a small two-room apartment when we were married. We had to catch a bus to go shopping for our one sack of groceries. There were no frills, but we loved each other. Love makes pork and beans and chicken soup taste like a five-course dinner. That love still works the same way after sixty-four years.

ENJOY YOUR WORK

I almost put "Love Your Work" as a title to this. "Love" is thrown around so much I decided not to further belittle the word. The idea of love still carries a higher meaning to me than the way this world regurgitates it at every turn. If you don't have enthusiasm and joy in what your work, funds will be scarce as hen's teeth. Enjoying the big picture of what we are doing, no matter what the work is, eliminates many battles. Many times, it alone will win the war.

Stephen King, one of the most successful writers of our day, said that he never wrote for the money or fame. He writes because he likes to write.

We may not agree with his subjects or content but we can't argue with the principle. If you don't really like where you are or what you are doing, you are a flop at all of it. Leave it and get busy doing what you like to do. Many think it is a great virtue to continue what they hate doing, complaining and griping in misery. The Bible records only one Noah, but I somehow believe even he enjoyed preaching to hardheads and working with gopher wood.

I met a man at the small airport in Iloilo City, Philippines. We've known each other for over twenty years. He used to pastor a church but for the past five years has been in mission work. Beaming, he said, "I've never had so much fun!" I remember him being as sour and sober as a judge when he pastored. His enthusiasm is contagious now.

Recently in a small church in Kentucky where it is evident the "going is rough as a cob" the pastor stirred me with his enthusiasm and plans for the church. He will make it because his excitement will knock the rough places off the cob.

Learning to keep your eye on the major goal stirs enthusiasm. All work has unpleasant tasks. The teacher may not enjoy grading papers until 2 A.M. or hearing an irate parent gripe about Johnny's detention. But the day of graduation makes it all seem like nothing. A pastor may not enjoy the magic moments of marriage ceremonies where foolish people spend thousands of dollars on flowers, rehearsal dinners, and clothes, to only wait for all of it to be thrown down the divorce drain two years later. But looking at those who survived years of trouble and work, still sitting together in church, make a few miscues bearable. Digging postholes and stringing wire are nothing when you look at the finished fence.

Several years ago I built our family a house. Sore muscles, hammered fingers, and can to can't hours faded into forgetfulness when I saw the satisfaction on the faces of my wife and children.

Things don't always work right. I'm writing this portion sitting in our place on the island of Panay in the Philippines. The water and power was on when I went to bed. The Flowers De Mayo fiesta music on the streets blared through our room until 2 A.M. After 2 hours of sleep, I looked forward to the cool morning shower to relieve the sweaty 90-degree heat of a miserable night. I also looked forward to my morning cup of coffee. But when I got up, the power was off. Stumbling around at 430 A.M. with my flashlight, I decided on a glass of water and to wait until daylight for my shower. The power came on at 5 A.M. and I got up for my shower. Guess what, no water. Now the power is on but the water is off, and no shower is in sight. Enjoyable? In a couple of hours we travel to visit a village church pastored by one of our Filipino graduates. It is in a poor place and a piggery is adjacent to the building. The pigs will be my cover! No one will ever know. The satisfaction of seeing the church and pastor make the loss of power and water seem like nothing. Far better to be here stinking like a pig and being a part of the work of God in a hard place than to be in the First Church, smelling of hairspray and cologne with everyone as dead as a doornail.

I look at the Philippines and see a missionary family. I gaze towards China and see three missionary families. In Mexico I see a missionary family. I turn to the West Coast and see a pastor. There are many others.

The long four years of Bible school hours on Monday and Tuesday nights (after a regular day of pastoral duties) now seem a small price for such a reward. I look at my former church where I labored for seventeen years and see the man I had the privilege to train as its pastor. The church is going strong. Keep your eye on the big picture.

Nothing dulls enthusiasm like forgetting the victories and experiences of the past. Force yourself to remember how God is faithful to you. All of the past is part of the future. Most of what God did in the past was to prepare you for the future. Forget your failures but evaluate your mistakes and determine to not repeat them. Moses, Joshua, and Paul always reminded themselves and others of what God did in the past. When it seems nothing is happening, the ship is dead in the water, or the clock has stopped, force yourself to remember God's faithfulness to you.

Assuming you like what you are doing in the first place, all of these will help you keep enthusiasm in your work. Keep your eye on the big picture and always head toward that goal; accept the fact that if things can go wrong, they will; and above all, remind yourself of God's faithfulness when dullness or deadness creeps in. If all those fail to encourage you, load up the family and get away for a few days. When you return you may have a different attitude.

GOALS

Money goals are not the goals you want to emphasize. A proper ministry produces the money for it. The problem is not to raise money. The problem is how to define, justify, set and meet the intermediate steps to reach a ministry goal. Get a man's heart and his pocketbook comes with it. If you can convince the church the need really exists, they will do it for you.

First of all define and justify the main goal, or better yet, let somebody in the congregation do it for you. For example, the church lighting is not sufficient. The lights are fifty years old and the auditorium is dark. The worst thing you can do is get up one Sunday morning and decide you are going to ramrod the project through if it harelips the devil. You muster up all the pastoral authority you can and pronounce from the pulpit that God "spoke to you about the lights." First of all, that's a lie, and second, everybody knows it. *You* might be the only one who has ever thought about it or even cares about it.

You have to be part farmer in these matters on spending money. Plow the ground, break the clods, make the rows, plant the seed, water the crop, and reap the harvest. It is not done overnight, but it will happen without a church split. This is true whether you have money in the bank or you have to take special offerings over and above the budget to pay for the lights.

Plow the ground. Make subtle remarks from time to time (not every week) about how dark the auditorium is. Magnify the need every time an opportune problem presents itself regarding the old lights. Bulbs are sometimes difficult to find or replace in old light fixtures. Next time Mr. Joe is changing the bulbs be there to help and to remind him what a difficult job he has with those old light fixtures.

If you have some older folks who need more light to read, apologize for the dim lights on the church's behalf. Get you a pulpit light because "you can't see your Bible under the old lights." Mention (in a sensitive way) from the pulpit any complaints about the lights.

Within a few months we needed a new auditorium at the "broke church" mentioned above.

Along with it we needed additional restrooms and a paved parking lot but we didn't have the money in the bank to do any of it. So I started plowing and breaking down the clods of opposition.

The former pastors led the church in a massive bond program to buy land and build a new building. The week before we arrived at the church, the new building burned to the ground and the State Fire Marshall cried, "Arson!" All the deacons took a lie detector test and passed. The former pastor refused. The insurance company refused to pay and the local bondholders were asking for their money back. To say the least, it was a touchy situation.

Here's the picture. The church is $350,000 in debt and no money is in the bank. Offerings and school tuition combined can't meet the bills, and the church's reputation is tarnished in the community. Thirty-five people have to do something about it. Somehow I believed we could do it and I enjoyed the challenge.

I placed a few conditions on the church if I was to be their pastor. I wrote out what I expected from them and required one hundred percent agreement by the deacons. I required them to allow me complete freedom with finances and preaching. What was spent and what was paid, and where I preached and how often I was gone, I would determine. This sounds like a dictatorial stance. It was. But even in that, I knew I had to be a compassionate dictator.

Some practical reasons impelled me to do this. First, I knew the finances of the church could not meet my family's needs.

I could preach Bible conferences on Thursdays or Fridays or help some Christian Schools during the week. I also needed the time in other places to keep me fired up. Plus, I did not need any long protracted deacon's meetings questioning why we spent money on the obvious. I did not make the agreement *after* I took the church; it was my condition <u>before</u> I went. What other choice did they have? I was the only idiot who would take such a mess. They agreed and we moved. The ability to make quick, on the spot decisions without waiting to have a committee or deacon meeting, is a priority issue when you are dealing with urgent matters.

I determined to not preach on money or giving, the exact opposite of what is usually done. I preached doctrinal messages on who God is and what He does. I did not buy the latest book on raising money written by big time preachers. Instead, I read what successful business people did. *I did not speak on giving money in any message for five years.* I emphasized character and honesty from the pulpit and used every Bible example of how God led His people through hard times. In other words, we concentrated on developing confidence and inspiring people.

Break up the big goal into smaller, attainable ones. This doesn't mean to write them out on a board and have everyone memorize them. Have them fixed in your mind and move towards them. Adjust or scrap them as necessary, but always move towards the big picture.

I wanted a positive message in all areas. I didn't want every Sunday School class to hear all about the past church trouble every Sunday. Enough of that gossip went on during the week.

We disbanded all teen and adult classes and I taught one "Auditorium Sunday School Class." We continued the nursery and children's classes. It is hard to concentrate when little Betsy has a wet diaper or the toddlers are crawling under the pews.

We had to put some life into the regular scheme of services. We eliminated the useless reports after Sunday School of attendance, offerings, etc. We also removed the "brag" board on the front wall listing number of Bibles brought, those on time, those present last week, and offerings. I looked at every practice and if it did not serve a real need, we cut it out. Services were streamlined. Announcements were short and sweet. We did not sing thirty minutes; we sang a maximum of three hymns. The main menu was Bible teaching in every service.

We set the Sunday evening service for 6 P.M. *(an unheard-of thing at that time and it was not to go home and watch TV — it gave me longer to preach on Sunday evenings)*. On Sunday mornings I preached salvation and practical Christian living messages. On Sunday evenings I got more sensational and drew chalk pictures along with a message on current events and the Bible. On Wednesday evenings I began going through a New Testament book verse by verse. After seventeen years we taught through every New Testament book from the pulpit, verse by verse, except Matthew. Almost all of the Old Testament books were taught.

We began to teach that if you are a church member, you are responsible to be at every meeting of the church. There is nothing special about Sunday morning from 11A.M. -Noon.

Monday night is as important as Sunday morning. The Lord is "in His holy temple" (the body of the believer) twenty-four hours a day, seven days a week. If you are a church member, you are supposed to be in the church when it meets. One of the killers of church life is to teach or give the impression that "church worship services" on Sunday morning is more important than serving Him on Tuesday afternoon.

I brought quality preachers who said worthwhile things in the pulpit for special meetings. Men that could say something without taking all day to say it. Some preachers are jealous of "their" pulpit to the point of only having speakers who are somewhat less in ability than themselves. The preacher feels inadequate and wants to protect his image. Get the most effective speakers, men who are doing something. You and the church will benefit from it.

We had Bible conferences and groups of pastors from other places. When I set the meeting schedule, I put the least effective speakers in the lessor time slots and kept their time on a firm, short schedule. The men who were successful examples and able to communicate were scheduled for the main services.

We showed films and videos-sometimes on Sunday evenings. You have to get the holy starch out of your pants if you are going to get folk's attention.

Set small attainable goals that move the church towards the end you wish. Be willing to change and adapt the goals to meet the people's ability. As you reach some of those goals, the church is developing confidence in doing what they thought could never be done. Don't be afraid to try innovative things, as long as they move you toward the main goal.

BUDGET ADJUSTMENTS

On practical day by day economics, we went to each of the bondholders and personally promised them we would pay them back every cent with interest. We went to those we owed money and promised the same. Keep in mind that the church could have called it quits, declared bankruptcy, and the few members scattered to other churches in the neighborhood. To their credit they did not.

I emphasized the fact that the school was a ministry of the church, not a separate entity. We met with the teachers and promised we would make it. I set a rule for myself that only church members would work in the school. I did not run in and fire everybody that did not agree with me. As the non-members left, we hired only church members. Some of the best teachers are not college graduates, but church moms with a burden for Christian education. We only had K to 6th grades but I set a goal for a full school. Enrollment when I began was around fifty and when I left seventeen years later it was K-12 with over three hundred students, thirty staff members with plenty of classrooms and a full gym. We accomplished this mostly by growing our own students and only adding grades when we could afford it. There were times when I taught classes because we had no one else or could not afford another teacher.

We also cut the "fluff." Every item we could cut from the budget, we did. We concentrated on the essentials to keep operating and did without the other.

I simplified the budget into broad categories. School tuition and church offerings were combined to meet the needs. Expenses were handled the same way.

On the income and expense lines I kept them separate but in practice we could use any money in the one church checking account to pay any bill. Since the school used all the facilities every day, this was easy to justify. The school was a challenge in itself and I'll have to include all those battles in another book.

To deal with the insurance company, we enlisted the help of the most hard-nosed, common sense businessman in the church. After several months he eventually got the insurance company to pay up and we were relieved of the bond debt. Get the right man to do the job and it will be done right.

The problem is not money in any situation. Most people waste enough money every week on junk to handle any church need. The problem is for the pastor to eliminate useless and traditional church operations, convince the people of the real needs to reach the big goal, and get them involved in meeting those needs.

REACH OUT TO THE CHURCH

Above all, get involved in people's lives outside the pulpit. Funds for the work do not come in many cases because the members do not know the pastor, and the pastor does not know them. Don't be afraid to let them learn you put your pants on the same way they do -- one leg at a time. By the very nature of your office, you are isolated from people in the church. You must find a way to get with your membership outside the pulpit, especially the men. Talking to folks from the pulpit only is the slowest way to get anywhere.

Every few weeks we had "eating meetings", potluck dinners on the grounds, right after the morning service. At other times we would get together and have a fish fry or a Rook tournament. My wife is an excellent cook and can put a meal for twenty on the table within thirty minutes. We had several families at our home many times for fellowship meals. Most of the time we had the whole church. Those meals and my wife's hospitality abilities probably did more to build the church than all my preaching. Later, we had too many members to do it. When I had a good family prospect, we would have them over for dinner and my wife's "new member" dessert. We jokingly said that once you ate it, you had to join the church. And I believe it worked. One hundred percent that ate, joined.

I went after men, not women. I tried not to offend the cooks, but a church that gets anything done must grab the men first. Get the man and you have the whole family. Keep the prissing and effeminate stuff out of the pulpit and preach hard to the men. On Sunday tell them they are lazy and sorry and no good and then go fishing with them during the week. They will appreciate you for telling the truth and their wives will amen the subject.

I got together with the key men of the church and new prospects at every chance I could. I love to fish but hate to hunt. I froze my butt off many mornings on deer hunts just to build a church. I would stand around the fire after the hunt and listen to who heard what and where the signs were — and I tried to act interested. I love to fish and I concentrated on that. I went fishing with almost every man in the church, those that could and those that couldn't. The man who is pastoring the church right now is one of the best fishermen I've ever seen and he taught me most of what I know about bass fishing.

You need a time when you can systematically teach the Bible outside regular pulpit hours. Pastors commit a major error in neglecting this avenue or turning it over to others. *People who attend extra hours Bible teaching are a major source of ministry support for the pastor, if he is the teacher.* Allegiances are developed in a small group that meets for Bible study. There is a bond between student and teacher that can not be developed elsewhere.

Within a few weeks after my arrival we announced the beginning of Open Bible College on Monday and Tuesday evenings from 630 P. M. to 930 P.M. This enabled me to have a forum other than Sunday morning and evening. I said if we had at least seven students show up we would start it. We had eleven.

I accepted black students in the Bible school as well as the Christian day school—another no-no in the South at that time, and received some flack because of it. This was in central Alabama in the 1970's. You can imagine how popular I was with the ministerial association and the "good ol' boys" in town. Those black graduates are among my best friends today.

The Bible school enabled me to personally teach and train Sunday School teachers as well as many of the future staff. Within four years I had an excellent base of church leadership. They gradually took places of leadership in the church. This one thing is the best move we made as far as establishing a strong foundation for future growth. It was not because I realized at the time all the future benefits. This was one of many things the Lord just threw in, despite my ignorance. By the grace of God this happened,

There are several men pastoring churches in the USA and foreign countries, and seven missionaries on foreign fields who graduated from that school.

Many other graduates are teaching the Bible in churches and Bible schools.

The Bible school is still in operation. It will continue---IF the principles that built it continue.

Raising money is one of the more touchy issues in church work. Mine was intensified is this case due to the previous pastor. If the people can spend some time with you, it will help you to speak more sensibly from the pulpit, stay on major issues, and seem more practical in their eyes. Personal time out of the pulpit with people will also cover any misunderstandings that arise from our many faults in preaching. Like the little girl said after a sermon, "Daddy, was he just preaching, or did he mean it?"

REACH OUT TO THE WORLD

Most pastors wear themselves out and waste their time on visitation that never works. You may be a great personal soul winner, and if you are, by all means go get 'em. But most pastors are not the best for initial contacts. They read a book on soulwinning by someone like Rick Warren or Jack Hyles and think they can do the same. You can, if you have his personality and ability. But if you are like most of us, you had better do what you can do. Saul's armor did not suit David. I discovered the most ineffective thing for me was general visiting on Thursday evening. I also discovered it was the most ineffective thing most of the members did. Arrive at the front door on Thursday evening and announce you are from –Baptist Church and you get a horselaugh because they know about the fights in the churchyard a few months before.

The big job I had was to get the gospel out to the town, State, and around the world. But I was up to my hips in alligators. Some things had to be taken care of right away, and no time could be wasted on unproductive efforts. We had to utilize the things that worked for us at the time. We also had to plan so as to be more effective and stable in the future.

Over the years I have tried every trick in the book to get people out on Thursday or Saturday morning visitation. Threats, meals, awards—you name it and I've done it. The Bible does not say the pastor is responsible to reach the community. That is every Christian's job.

I began to emphasize to the whole church that each one was to do what he or she could to get the gospel out. At work and play, we are to be witnesses for Christ. I challenged the members to invite those they worked with or shopped with to church or special services. It worked. Soon we had relatives and acquaintances saved and regular in church. I stopped pushing Thursday night visitation. We continued it for many years and I went, but I visited "hot" prospects on Thursday night. Those parents in the school or those who visited with us the previous Sunday were my best contacts.

Examine what you are doing with regard to winning the lost and reaching new members. If it doesn't work, drop it. Intensify what does work.

We had street, jail, and nursing home ministries. But I let those develop in a natural way. As the Lord led some to go to the jails, I encouraged them. But I did not try to put a guilt trip on those who did not. If a man had a nursing home ministry, I encouraged him but did not brow beat others to go.

TACKLING FACILITY PROBLEMS

The church was at first meeting in the old, stripped building, which they had tried to sell after the new one was built, but was unsuccessful. Thank God it did not sell. At least we had a building to meet in. We had three areas: a half-underground educational building, a small nursery and office area, and the auditorium. All of it was concrete block with flat roofs and tied together in the most impractical way and all roofs leaked.

We were sitting on folding chairs in the auditorium block building with a flat roof. A long rain brought out the buckets at strategic places. The lay in ceiling tiles got soaked and collapsed. We tried quick fix methods on the roof but it was so old, ten new leaks sprung up every time we fixed one. I must have personally put 100 gallons of tar patch on the roof before I got an idea to enlist some help. I formed an unofficial roof crew every time we had to repair the roof.

One of the most ineffective things you can do is to try the job *all by yourself.* The second most ineffective thing is to *let others do it all.* You must enlist help but get in there with them and sweat. Every able-bodied man soon spent time on the roof in blistering summer heat and the roof became the main topic of conversation. I apologized to the visitors for the buckets under their feet and listened to the members' suggestions on where "that new leak was coming from." Some of my men began to talk about devils in that roof. I encouraged it. One or two of them saw stopping the leaks once for all as a personal challenge to their manhood. All I had to do was enlist my roof crew each week and wait. The ground was plowed; most of the clumps broken down, and the seed was planted and watered--literally.

It took about a year but finally funds came in to put a sloped roof on over the flat one. Our leaking problem was fixed but now we had a new one. Attendance increased to about a hundred and more folding chairs had to be bought. Soon the old auditorium was crowded. Some of the kids sat on the floor. We bought some infernal church pews. I hate them with a passion. They are the most overpriced, ill-designed, uncomfortable seats in the world. I've often thought if I ever pastored another church, I'd have rocking theater seats with cup holders, not for grape juice but for coffee and cokes. The pews didn't solve our seating problem for long. We had to have more space, but our needs were bigger than our pocketbook.

We needed a jolt in the arm. I took a shoebox out of my daughter's closet, wrote $22,000 on it and set it on the holy communion table Sunday morning. If we had at least twenty-two slips of folded paper with a name indicating a $1,000 dollars on each one within two weeks, we would begin a new auditorium on top of the flat educational building. If we didn't have at least twenty-two, we would burn the paper without ever looking at the names. There were twenty-five within two weeks. We were able to purchase the steel frame and start a new auditorium with that amount. Another step in the right direction.

When we began tearing off the old roof in preparation for the concrete floor and frame, there were about twenty church men working every afternoon until dark. I was right there with them. When we framed up the interior and ran he ductwork for the heating and AC system, I didn't know anything about building but I was there.

The church members did the majority of every building we built and I was ignorant but right in the middle of all of it. We subbed out the technical stuff but did every thing we could to cut the costs. As a pastor, I got double benefits from that work; we got the buildings done at a fraction of cost and I got to know my members in a close and personal way.

We disbanded all committees. My practice is to do what is needed and leave the rest of it alone. Why set up meetings or committees just to have something to do? We had deacons meetings when there was a need. There were no school committees, missionary circles, or flower committees. When a person came to me with an idea about something "we" needed to paint or nail, I made him chairman of the board right then and there. That stops useless or ill-timed suggestions.

ORGANIZATION AND STAFF

Organization should be based on as simple structure as possible. Endless chains of command are cumbersome, confusing, and ineffective. At the beginning, we were simply pastor and church. Later, as the work grew and more organizational structure was necessary, we added what worked.

Church staff was added only after they proved themselves as church members. This kept us from a multitude of problems. I hired a couple of people from the outside over the seventeen years and paid dearly for doing it. In both instances we were faced with what we thought was a need. It is better to let the need exist than hire a stranger. Resumes and character references are not enough proof of a person in church work.

From the beginning, I had the greatest secretary a pastor could hope for. She knew how I thought and could cover any situation. Without her I seriously doubt I could have done much at all. She worked at a fraction of the pay she should have received. I tend to lose everything I should keep and my desk looks like a tornado disaster area. She was orderly and knew where everything was located. One of many talents she had was to be able to give me any church member's telephone number without a moment's hesitation. Her husband was a deacon in the church and both of them excelled as faithful church members.

God also gave me a great co-worker in my school principal. It was miraculous how he came to the position. He was a member when I first came to the church but after a few years his secular job moved him to another state. He always had a burden for the school ministry and was a tremendous help before he left. One day he was on my heart. I needed a school principal. The school was growing and I could not keep up with the day by day responsibilities it required. So, I called him on the telephone. At he very moment I called him, he had just been in a strenuous job meeting. As a result, God worked out many things and he returned to the church as our school principal. He stayed with me for the remainder of my pastorate there and is a dear friend. We worked long and hard hours on school problems and building problems. Every building we built has our marks in and on it, from laying tile to nailing two by fours. His wife is also one of the most effective elementary teachers I have ever seen. They poured their lives into the work and God has blessed them for it.

After a few years my associate pastor came. I had the honor of training him in the Bible. He worked at a regular job and was faithful in all areas before he ever became associate pastor.

After accepting the position, he continued to work and support himself but made the ministry his main concern.

He is one of the most faithful men and helped me for over eight years as my associate. Years before, I knew he was going to pastor some church and be successful at it. I prepared him as my "Timothy" to take the work when I got too old or left the church. I really never planned to leave the church. My major purpose was to prepare him to take the ministry if something happened to me, or at least to take a part of the work as it continued to grow. God burdened my heart for missions and then I understood what my associate was trained to do—he would continue the work of the church while we would move into mission work. He has been the pastor of the church since we left years ago. He has done so in an honorable and effective way. I often say he is a better pastor than I ever was, and I mean that.

God gave me some men who really took the work to heart. Time fails me to tell you of all these. Almost every man in the church gave himself to the work. A few of the men worked long hours at their job and then worked ten hours on church projects several nights a week. The handful that were critics, I ignored. As long as a critic did not affect the work in any significant way, I let him be. I won some of them and churched a few over seventeen years.

I made many mistakes and made a fool out of myself more than once. I had no inside track with God. The only thing that is perfect on this earth is the Holy Bible. To the degree any person follows it, God blesses. I was a sinner saved by grace, trying to serve the Lord and learning as I went. Most of the folks saw me as more than a pastor. They saw me as a friend who entered into their troubles with them. When I made a fool of myself, they were convinced I had not done a permanent job.

You might wonder what all of the above have to do with raising money. These are not your usual topics. Actually, they are the producers of funds. I am sure that the work we did is not perfect. I am positive it could have been done much more effectively. But from my small understanding, it was not preaching on money that did anything. If we did it right, to the degree we did it, the funds were there to meet the need. Someone said that if you find what people want and then give it to them at a fair price, they will buy it.

Money is not produced by visualization. Money does not come to us in order to find something to do with it. Money comes because there is something we are doing that is worthwhile.---Dave Reese

WILD PIGS, RIDES AND CUTS IN MINDANAO PHILIPPINES

We departed from Iloilo to Mindanao aboard the Fokker 50 plane and arrived in General Santos City about 2 hours and forty minutes later. There are two weekly flights direct from Iloilo to General Santos, on Tuesday and Sunday. General Santos has a new airport, but it is still in the stages of development in 1999.

In General Santos we went to Lea's Pension House, a place to stay the night before going to the mountain. Prices are 450 pesos (USD $15) for the economy double and 250 pesos for the standard single.

We washed up and got refreshed. Leaving the ladies to rest, we went to a believer's house to make plans for the next day to the mountain. On the way back we stopped at the Shumart Store and got some water and supplies for the mountain.

Jerry A., another of our graduates and pastor of a new work in the jungle, shows up at the hotel and we talk a while about the work. He came down the mountain the previous day and arranged for a truck, an old military weapons carrier, to carry us to Tulale.

The next morning, after a good rest, we meet the vehicle downstairs at 5AM. Raphael drives all of us to Isulan, a town about 70 miles northwest of the city at the foot of the mountains. We get to the place where the truck is to meet us and find that the owner "has an emergency" and therefore the truck is not available. Nothing new!

We drive over to the market area and after some discussion, a large six-wheeled vehicle is declared to be our new transportation at a price of only 1500 pesos round trip. The original truck was to have cost 2000 pesos, so we are assured the new truck is a bargain. Everything is "better" than before even though we waste three hours finding a new vehicle. However, before we leave the owner tells me the price is 2000 since the first truck owner had contacted this one to help us out.

We notice this truck is loaded with supplies and rice for the people and little shops along the way. After about 15 stops up the mountain it became clear my 2000 pesos is just extra money for the driver at no cost to him. Sue and the other lady ride in the cab with the driver. One of the ladies wonders the whole 3-hour trip why her seat is so warm. Come to find out, she sat on the driver's hot rice lunch all the way up the mountain. Roger, Jerry and I ride in the open bed back on sacks of rice with about twenty other hitchhikers.

We arrived at the top of the mountain but we are still about 5 miles from Tulale. We stop at a guard station. This is a guard who works for a Chinese man who bought thousands of acres of land throughout the mountains. Without permission no one goes up the road. The man is cutting the forest but we have no interference in the political or ecological issues in the PI. Susan A., our Bible woman in Tulale, has been going to the Chinese man's house where the foreman and workers' families live. She is teaching them to read and giving them a gospel witness. Because of that, we can pass.

Unfortunately, when we arrive at the gate, a guard not familiar with the orders from his boss, is on duty. He looks formidable with the AK-47 over his arm. He radios his headquarters in Isulan. After a 30-minute wait and a lot of static from the 2 way radio, he lifts the gate and we go up the small one lane muddy road to Tulale.

We arrive in the village. It is about 2pm, eight and one-half hours after we left General Santos City. The truck stays overnight and is to leave the next afternoon, collecting sacks of corn along the way from various farmers to trade for rice and other products in town.

After exchanging greetings with our graduate and pastor, Franklin and Alma P., their children, Alfran and Ivan, Virgie E. and Susan A., our Bible women, and Melchor S., Franklin's assistant, we have lunch of bananas, rice, and adobo chicken.

The village children play and sing as they remember us from previous visits. The neatness of the mission houses and church is very impressive. Even though this is remote jungle, flowers are planted all around the church and houses. Bougainvillea, African daisies, roses, Impatiens, marigolds, orchids, along with several plants noted for their medicinal value in teas and poultices, cover the area.

We rest for about an hour and prepare for the prayer services at the church. I speak on Romans 5:19: "For as by one man's disobedience many were made sinners, so by the obedience of one shall many be made righteous." I am determined to tell as much of a story as I can, beginning with God creating man, man sinning and Jesus coming to pay for man's disobedience. Roger B. interprets as I preach, so I speak simply and concisely.

Darkness begins to fall and the village gasoline corn sheller is started and its alternator powers the 12-volt lights. The lights in the building—two of them—are on for the special occasion. Children with smudged faces sit on the dirt floor at my feet. Every bamboo seat is taken in the building. The dirt floor, bamboo pews, and faces peering through the open windows give a special flavor to this prayer meeting. The people listen intently to the message. Only one or two Bibles are among all the people. At the invitation 22 people come forward to receive Jesus Christ as their Savior.

After services we meet with all our workers in Susan A's house. We read the Bible by the oil light and pray for the work of reaching other villages with the gospel. The meeting and prayer finished we all settle for the night. Sue and I stay in one of the small 8' X 5' rooms of the nipa hut, our visitors in the other, and Susan and Virgie in the front room.

As Sue and I lay on our backs on the hard rattan mat, I switch on my flashlight in order to check the thatched roof above our heads for any unwanted guests. (Susan had killed a snake in the other room a few days earlier.) Three things are quite essential before you sleep in the jungle — I've learned this from experience. One, know where you are and as much as possible, know what and who are around you. Second, close all your bags and leave nothing open for unwanted guests to crawl into. Third, be sure your flashlight is where you can grab it in a second. Sometimes, I simply sleep on it as I did this night.

Soon the oil lights and flashlights are out and all is quite. About thirty minutes after all was quite, a lot of shouting came from across the way. We jump up, pull on our pants and run outside to see what is going on. One of the men had killed a wild pig. He gestures to show how he had worn his flashlight (it was "supped-up" with two extra cells tied with wire to the regular four cells) on his head. He had taken one shot and got the pig.

Various villagers poke the pig, look at his teeth, and comment on how it was shot. The story is told in T'boli about ten times. They remind me of Alabama deer hunters, telling what they saw, heard, tracks in the ground, rubbings, and in general, spending more time talking about how it happened than actually doing it. I guess it makes the meat better. It reminds me that men are pretty much the same all over the world. After the news is told again and again, we go back to bed. There is a nip in the air and our long johns are not quite enough for the cold jungle night in a breezy bamboo hut. You feel so foolish hauling long johns around in your bags at the bottom of the mountains in 98-degree heat but mountain temperatures at night drop into the 50's.

The next morning, well before daylight, voices awakened us — not loud-but subdued. I am cold anyway, so I get up to stand by the fire as the men clean the pig, chickens, and turkey.

The ladies are preparing the other food for the Thanksgiving Day Service. Thanksgiving day is not as in the USA — it is simply a day set aside by the churches to give thanks for all of God's blessings. Usually, it corresponds somewhat to our southern tradition of "homecoming day." Former members come, a feast is prepared. One of the villagers from Pagunay (our newest work where Jerry A. is) had brought the live turkey. The gobbler stayed tied in a sack in the yard and constantly grumbled the whole evening until execution just prior to daybreak.

There were several instances when Sue helped the people with medical problems. Emelda C, one of the Bible women had been in the town at the base of the mountain and was returning to Tulale. The motorcycle had a wreck, throwing her and the others off and cutting her head. The cut is about 1-2" above and behind her ear. (Motorcycles driven by a man with five Filipinos on it is the standard way to travel up the mountain) Sue cleans the dirt and pebbles out and, instead of stitches, decides to butterfly the cut.

Another case is a man who, a week earlier cut the top of his foot just below the ankle with a machete. The foot is swollen, the 4" cut infected, and red streaks are running up his leg. Sue irrigates the wound, gets the pus out, applies Bactroban, and gives him penicillin. The next day, the streaks were gone and the foot swelling down. Sue probably saved his foot and possibly his life. He was going to tough it out as they do so many times. Several others are treated for fevers and respiratory infections.

The Thanksgiving Day services begin with songs and testimonies. Roger B. preaches and at the invitation, 12 come forward for salvation and 8 for full time Christian service. 4 of them want to go to Bible school at once, but 2 cannot read. So Susan, our Bible woman, enrolls them in her literacy class she teaches 4 days a week. The others will attend our Bible school in November.

The people come in their tribal dress for the services. Some come from huts out in the jungle away from the village. Beaded clothing, strings of beads around the neck, 5 to 20 earrings in each ear, many small bells around their waist that tinkle as they walk, and combs or headdresses of many small, rolled beads in their hair, furnish their decoration.

Children are everywhere. Now there are about 80 children and we need to build a room where they can be taught while the adults attend services.

The feast is served after church services with lots of rice, boiled wild vegetables, and some manok (jungle chicken) and baboy (the pig killed the day before). All eat in typical rural Filipino fashion, with their fingers. Some use a palm leaf as their plate.

The village leader informs us that a month earlier she had gone to Manila to represent the tribal people in that region before President Ramos. He asked her to do a tribal dance, which she did. I saw one of these dances on my first trip to Tulale in 1996. He also asked her if they still worshipped the wild dove. She told him, no, that now they had a Protestant missionary and church. She also told him of the medical and literacy classes provided by our workers. Before we left she gave us an invitation to come to the village anytime. We are always welcome, she said. Her adopted daughter wants to attend our Bible school next year.

We get on the corn truck and I throw my remaining candy to the children gathered around the truck as we roar off down the single lane rocky road toward the bottom of the mountain. Sue and other ladies are in the front with the driver and the rest of us are sitting on the sacks in the back.

We stop to pick up sacks of corn at several huts as we bounce down the trail to the town of Isulan below. A cobra someone had decapitated lies alongside the road. A tire goes flat in the middle of a thunderous downpour and are we soaked!

Three hours later we are in the town and thankful to see our truck waiting to carry us the next 2 hours to General Santos City.

That evening some dear Filipino believers in General Santos invited us to dinner at their house. They want to hear of the mountain work. To many Filipinos in the cities, jungle work is very interesting and mysterious to them. Many would never think of traveling to the mountains since Muslim rebels are everywhere, robbing or kidnapping anyone for ransom. We have chicken adobo, pork, a salad of melon, pineapples, bananas, and papaya with mayo along with soft shelled crabs and prawn and seafood soup. This is a real treat and I'm sure it cost them a lot to prepare such a meal for the five of us.

This is a typical visit to our Mindanao jungle churches. Now (2022) we have 85 of them. God is doing amazing things in these remote areas of the world. Why don't you consider joining us? If you can't go, will you help us go?

"Also I heard the voice of the Lord, saying, Whom shall I send, and who will go for us? Then said I, Here am I; send me." (Isaiah 6:8 KJB)   ---Dave and Sue Reese

PARENTAL DUTIES

Teach

"And thou shalt teach them diligently unto thy children, and shalt talk of them when thou sittest in thine house, and when thou walkest by the way, and when thou liest down, and when thou risest up." (Deuteronomy 6:7 KJB)

Shamefully, many Christian parents do not do this. Some do not read their Bible to know what to teach. The Bible tells us who is to teach and what to teach: parents are to teach Scripture. It is no wonder there are disobedient children who criticize their parents and have no respect for authority.

"I have no greater joy than to hear that my children walk in truth." (3 John 1:4 KJB)

Train

Parents have the responsibility to train their children.

"Train up a child in the way he should go: and when he is old, he will not depart from it." (Proverbs 22:6 KJB)

God tells parents to train up (repetitive positive teaching) a child. It is the duty of both parents to teach good manners and acceptable behavior by their own behavior. If you are a single parent, responsibility falls upon you.

"10 Ye *are* witnesses, and God *also*, how holily and justly and unblameably we behaved ourselves among you that believe:

11 As ye know how we exhorted and comforted and charged every one of you, as a father *doth* his children,

12 That ye would walk worthy of God, who hath called you unto his kingdom and glory." (1 Thessalonians 2:10-12 KJB)

Provide

"Behold, the third time I am ready to come to you; and I will not be burdensome to you: for I seek not yours, but you: for the children

ought not to lay up for the parents, but the parents for the children." (2 Corinthians 12:14 KJB)

God tells us parents to make provision for our children. We must provide for our children to be clean, fed, and with health care met. If an adult does not desire to do these basic things, it is my opinion you should not attempt a family at all. We need to educate our children so they can in turn, be responsible parents.

Many parents do not assume these responsibilities and therefore rear some ill-taught children. They are handicapped only because their parents failed. How can we expect a wholeness of character when children are malnourished due to parental failure?

ROWDY ROOSTERS

Since my last rooster report, several things of note have happened. First, after the demise of the main rooster, the Filipina managed to get three to take its place.

A rooster must go through a period of time to learn the art of crowing like a rooster should. I'm not sure of the exact length- it probably depends upon the individual rooster and the quality of his innards. Although I have not made a global study, in the Philippines this is a combination scream and guttural growl of several decibels designed to produce the greatest antagonism upon the human ear at the most helpless time. Here in the Philippines, roosters prefer the very early hours of the morning, anywhere from 2:32 AM to 5:30 AM. All roosters know by sheer instinct that this is the time when the sweaty, insect bitten, itchy human slips into the deep sleep essential for a rested body and sane mind. Being roosters, they are determined to disturb during this defenseless state.

At any rate, the Three Roosterteers mastered the art by September. They also were mysteriously drawn to the tree of their forefathers next to my ear. However, by the grace of God, a lightning bolt struck the tree outside our window. It shucked all the leaves, rusted Wilbert's radio antenna, fried several lizards, and killed the tree dead as a hammer. The roosters were left without a minaret. The only tragedy was that the three were not in the tree when the wrath of the Almighty fell.

All three promptly took up bedding outside the next room in a small palm tree, trying to outdo the other each morning. No doubt they were plotting and waiting for a spring leaf cover (which never comes in the tropics and was never to come) to return to my window tree. Even from their new home, the shrill, triplicate crows pierced the early morning peace of my room.

American visitors came to our mission house and with them, the answer to my plight. Of course due to no design of my own, the unknowing couple (like Ruth lighting on Boaz's field) just happened to be assigned the room next to the Three Roosterteers limb. Knowing the gracious hospitality of the Filipino, I knew their ears would be tuned to our guests' every whim and wish, eager to please. The bedding was in place. The floors were swept. Their dirty laundry was washed. The meals were toned down to accommodate the Western palate.

We waited while two nights passed in a miserable crowing fashion. At the breakfast table on the third morning I casually asked if our guests were disturbed during the night. Filipino ears twitched. Roger Bayona stopped pouring the Milo. Wilbert leaned toward the table. Loretta paused from scraping the rice pan. The loud, blessed answer rang throughout the room as my unwary guest answers, "We rested, but I was awakened very early by a flapping of wings and a rooster crowing." "Oh, that must have been THE ROOSTERS that disturbed you," I said, making sure everyone in the house understood the culprits' social security numbers. Everyone resumed his or her duties. We eat breakfast and politely comment on a variety of issues and plans for the day. Inwardly I smile, knowing that justice is about to be served.

During the late afternoon, two scrawny, yellow legs show over the edge of a kitchen pot. This evening we have chicken adobo. Instead of the usual trio for the next early morning serenade, there is only a duet. The following afternoon, I notice four legs in the pot for supper. There is no flapping or chicken sound in the palm tree this night. An occasional "gekko-o-o-o" is its only sound as a lizard makes his love call and goes to sleep at a reasonable hour.

ROOSTER REGIMENT

Having done in the feathered friends by the devious means mentioned above, peace swept over the realm for several weeks. But one day we noticed little A-frame structures on the lot adjoining our church property. 2'X 2' squares of plywood are propped against each other at one side and spread at the bottom to make small tent like buildings. Curiosity got the best of me. Gradually I see the unfolding plan of our Filipino neighbor — a rooster garrison!

These are field tents for a rooster fighting cock regiment. Although cockfighting is outlawed by most USA states, the Philippines is not so cock conscious. It is one of the most revered professions and bloody forms of gambling. A crowing, strutting, fighting cock is soon tethered to a little post around each wooden tent, 30 of them.

Now every morning is a cacophony of fighting cocks from 2 to 4 AM, each cussing his neighbor in the Gallus language, trying to outdo the other.

A present survey is to seek out which Philippine beast a cock fears most. We figure a little cardboard cutout of a fox (?) or King Cobra (?) running along the fence by means of a string will cause multiple fatal family heart attacks.

While doing my research I have discovered some startling facts. One is: there are approximately 4.5 million red foxes in the Philippines. According to those who study foxes, the red fox was introduced by the Spanish in 1874 for game hunting and biodiversity. They released a couple hundred red foxes in Cagayan and Nueva Vizcaya all on the north island of Luzon.

The brilliant Spanish also introduced the red fox to Palawan—a western Philippine Island and a part of the Visayas region where we are. Although I have never spotted one, red foxes bred so crazily that they became a very common animal in all areas of the Philippines.

According to Wikipedia the fox hunts endangered Filipino creatures like the Philippine forest turtle, Mindoro climbing rat, red-vented cockatoos and the Philippine porcupine. They have no natural predators on the island except the human. Surely, if they can eat a porcupine and navigate the quills, they will have no problem with the two spurs of a fighting cock. It was encouraging to find they have colonized all of Luzon and Palawan and some have been spotted in the Visayas region where we live.

Assuming the neighbor fighting cocks—by instinct—will fear the red fox, I am presently cutting out a cardboard silhouette to paint a red fox with a string in his nose.

MISSIONS AND THE CHURCH

It could be that when the present generation of Christianity is evaluated by some future writer, they will say, "Never have so many with so much done so little of their duty."

Almost 20 centuries have passed since the Lord Jesus Christ died for all men. *Two thousand years-730,000 days-17,520,000 hours-1,051,200,000 minutes* ticked off the clock,and there are still 3,000 languages without one Bible verse. At the same time there are over 300,000,000 people that have never even heard the Name, Jesus. Most of them have heard of Coca Cola. There are multiplied thousands of towns and villages where there is no historical record of any attempt at evangelization.

To add woe to misery, we are not advancing on the evangelization of growing populations in developing countries; we are losing ground. Missions in the 21st Century requires more specialty training than 20 years ago. We are still trying to reach the world with methods and training that were not effective during the past fifty years, and are even less so today.

The average church remains in the dark with regard to its understanding of the missionary task, economic and political factors in a changing world, and how to reach into foreign cultures. Many think of the Asian countries such as China as being in the same condition as the 1800's. Europe is viewed as it was in WWII. Missions information is limited to a missionary paperback book written fifty to a hundred years ago. Although unlimited information on all subjects is at our fingertips, we remain ignorant of the actual field conditions. Accessibility to the "ends of the earth" has never been easier, yet we are more homebound than ever before. Most Christians are unaware that governments and policies, unchanged for centuries and decades in the past, are rapidly adjusting to move into the world market and are radically different than the home perception.

Missionaries themselves, as a whole, have not improved the level of information as to where they are and what they are doing. A few even hide the "good" and dwell on the "bad" to impress supporters at home. Sad to say, the average monthly prayer letter from a missionary is the poorest form of information about missions. The missionary is "under the gun" to write something each month to his supporters or face losing financial support. Most missionaries are not writers. The great majority have never studied effective writing. Many can not turn on a computer. Some must depend on a person in the USA to take a month old handwritten letter, type it, maintain a mailing list, and send it out each month. The missionary goes for months or in some cases, years, not knowing the status of those supporting him.

Missionaries need specialty training for the task. But the course of preparation essentially remains the same as that of fifty years ago. The cause of missions is strangled by outdated, ineffective communication between church and missionary.

Many mission organizations and boards, supposedly helps ministries to the local church, operate ministries that rival the church, rather than compliment it. Communication and accountability methods to the church remain unchanged from those used decades ago.

In the USA, the growing and robust personal soul-winning efforts of 1940-1990 by independent churches is degenerated to a technological and psychological attempt to "hold the fort."

This book attempts to stir the reader to a renewed and informed effort in the task of world evangelization. It also seeks to inspire innovative mission methodology without sacrificing scriptural principles.

WHERE ARE WE?

Millions of Christians have lived and died. The job of world evangelization was not completed by them. There are millions of professing Christians living. There are many cities in America with a thousand churches. Many in the present generation have a smug and false sense of success as they ride on redesigned coattails of the unique pioneers who built these churches. For the most part, once strong, vibrant and growing churches are now static monuments of the founders. Real revivals are stories of the past. Individual Christians are more apathetic toward missions than ever before and, of course, churches are not different. A strange church mixture of money, psychology and competitive adaptation is desperately trying to cope with keeping old members and winning new ones.

Within the city limits of Jacksonville Florida, there are 1200 Independent Baptist Churches alone. This means that God "led" at least 1,000 preachers to this city, already with many churches, instead of the areas of the world where there massive populations and few churches. In one county of North Carolina, there are 87 Independent Baptist Churches. There are more fundamental Baptist preachers in Washington State with a population of less than 3,000,000 than there are fundamental missionaries of all brands in China alone, which has 450 times greater population. India has almost the same population as China, is growing, and its missionaries are few. it is difficult on one hand to understand how God "is not willing that any should perish," and on the other, how He can lead a preacher to establish another church where there are already hundreds. *The conditions above constitute a major problem for all who claim to be "new creatures" in Christ Jesus.*

FOUR PITFALLS OF MISSIONS
     There are many contributing factors but four major ones need be addressed.

     First of all, materialism with its cares of the world stifles the Christian's spirituality.
Secondly, missions demands old fashioned manpower work, and work in an affluent society is not popular. No amount of radio or TV or computer use will out perform a flesh and blood witness, standing eyeball to eyeball. We are not opposed to the above methods. This book is a product of a computer and modern print technology. But we are depending more and more on technology to replace *kneeology and footology and plain old common horse sense.*
Lastly, the church that attempts to carry out its mission responsibility without knowing the difference between the mission program of the kingdom and the mission program of the age of grace is crippled at best. These are at the core of much of the failure to carry out the Lord's command.

DEFINITIONS

CHURCH
     In this book, *church*, refers to a local assembly of believers. In dealing with specific problems, as much as possible, specific people must be addressed. It does not help to address these matters to "the body of Christ." That is too general for our purpose. The more involved local churches are in missions, the more we will get done. To the degree the local church is involved in missions, to the same degree mission work will advance. Unless we have an effective mission work as an essential part of and a natural outworking of local churches, world evangelization will be a concept talked about, but poorly done.

MISSIONS

The term *missions* is used in the general sense of world evangelization; it is an active effort on the part of the church to communicate the gospel of Jesus Christ to the world in every generation. Missions does not embody the general, and normal, day by day operation normally performed by a church. Sunday School, bus ministries, Christian schools, or Bible studies are not within our scope of missions.

WORLD EVANGELIZATION

World evangelization embodies the idea, "to every person in every generation." It is another way to say, missions. World evangelization is a job never completed since people are born into this world every second. When one village is evangelized, another is ready. World evangelization means an ongoing work in the same village. A church placed in a particular city or area does not mean the job of evangelization is completed. The church must actively preach the gospel in all areas of the city at all times and continue to do so. Training and motivation to do so must be the perpetual work of its leadership. Its membership must see that the reason for them being there is to continually preach the word to those around them. They must also see that in addition to their own city, they are responsible, to the same degree, to a lost world.

INDIGENOUS CHURCHES

A church that is not missions minded is not a Biblical church. *Missions minded* means the church understands the Biblical reasons for its beginning, existence, and continuing purpose, and is actively carrying out that purpose through Scriptural means.

MATERIALISM

The church today has more money than ever before in history. Its resources stagger the imagination.There is almost no limit on what it can do, and does, to lavish these fruits of prosperity upon itself. Buildings, large and small, sit idle during weekdays with their indoor fountains, alcoves, lounges, bookstores, coffee shops,...and decorated walls. Elaborate framed oil paintings of missionary heroes of the past are in dominant positions but the small number of current missionary letters are hidden somewhere in a "missions" notebook. If there are multipurpose buildings, they came into existence for the purpose of keeping the church out of the "worldly" community programs.Instead of carrying the gospel and its influence into the community battlefield, the church retreated *from the high ground of integration with people in daily life* to monastery walls. Vehicles which serve no nobler purpose than carrying the Senior Citizens to the outlet mall once a year, or juniors to camp during the summer, line the church grounds. Out on the curbside, a large sign, blinking and bragging, proclaims "Building for the Glory of God." Closeby the walls rise on a new auditorium designed to seat twice as many as the present one. The present one is only half filled on Sunday evening and the church down the sreet just completed a new auditorium as well. The opposite side of the sign blindly preaches to slow givers to the new project, "Stingy giving is living as though there is no tomorrow." Churches have world wide web sites and put more money into setup, operation, and maintenance of the sites than they do in support of missions. Singing groups recruit pastors and members to gospel cruise trips and haul away offerings to buy higher decibel sound equipment for their psychological sessions of emotional frenzy.

When we use the term, missions, we actually are referring to world evangelization. God said to that early church, "Go ye into all the world and preach the gospel to every creature..." They understood it so literally that they saw it of more importance than personal luxeries and desires. They understood they were "ambassadors" of heaven, sent by the Christ who was coming back again to reckon with His servants as to what they had done with their responsibility. The more urgent task of winning souls to Jesus Christ took precedence over buildings, church furniture, color of carpet and the vagary of distractions some churches are mired in today. There is certainly nothing wrong with buildings and carpet. But there is something wrong when we spend more time and money on them than on our efforts to get the gospel out to a lost world.

The circle from apathy to apostasy is seen too often. A church begins with a few members and little material resources. In the early days there is a passion for souls, a burning desire to reach a lost community, and soon a small band gathers. There are no "programs" 'seminars" or fancy buildings. Seats are more than likely just folding chairs. The attraction is the gospel and the simplicity of the church purpose. Soon, more money is available because membership increases and with it, the offerings. Instead of channeling the funds as it did at the first, the church begins to make its existence easier and its services more attractive to the public. *There was nothing to attract them but the preaching of the cross at the beginning.* New buildings are built. Expensive church furniture which costs ten times more, replaces the folding chairs. The hymnbooks are embossed, decorations are added, special programs to compete with the world's social programs are added, and soon people are coming because the church has a ball team or facilities which rival any in town.

The pastor begins to marvel that so many are eager to go to camp, cookouts, vacations, or a ball game but so few attend a Monday night revival meeting. In order to get them to come to short sessions of preaching the word, added attractions like singing groups or spectacular demonstrations of men tearing telephone books in half must be attached to the preaching. The pastor weeps tears when families he has labored over for years joins the church down the road because 'they have a youth program" or some other social attraction. However, crowds beget crowds and the church goes on to plateau out. Then, the church looks at other churches and what they are doing "to reach the community" and, in order to be competitive, builds a bigger and better than their neighbor.

This cycle of selfish energy consumes the life of the church. There is no thought for millions in the world who do not have 1/1000 of the opportunity to hear the gospel as those in this city. Competitive churches line the streets of the USA cities while in cities and villages around the world, Jesus just as well should never have died--for there is no one who will come and tell them the gospel. Those who have the message and means to tell them are arguing over the cost of building a bigger church than the one down the street, or the color of carpet, or when the ball team will get to practice.

There are no funds available for real missions now. Justifying spending at home, the church says "We must have a strong home church first" and throws a small amount into the missionary pool. It looks for every opportunity to excuse itself from the call of the lost worldwide.

In order to continue its present course, *it must* justify its actions. Undue expectations in the form of missionary questionnaires, who a missionary associates with, where he/she went to school, demands that a certain number of souls be saved each year or churches built, all of these and a hundred more are laid on the missionaries' backs in order to justify *not sending* support to a missionary. Normal responsibility of the home ministry is classified as *missions* so the financial paper will look like a lot is spent on missions.

There is no time for missions or missionaries. "Give us a recap of your past 4 years work in 5 minutes." If there is a missions emphasis of any kind, it is relegated to one week a year. Missions is supposed to be the reason and life of the church; it is not one compartment of church activity among many.

Born out of the very missions heart of God, the average church denies its parental background and turns like a rebel child to the ways of the world. It is rich and increased with goods in the eyes of itself and the world, and does not know it is poor and blind and naked in the sight of God.

While this grim picture is true in many areas, there are a few churches that still maintain the balance between material prosperity in an affluent society and the responsibility to reach the world with the gospel. In almost every case, the pastor is a person who educated himself regarding missions in spite of the general examples of failure in the major chuches around him. For these churches, we thank God. Without them, the picture would be much worse.

WHO WILL GO FOR US?

People are God's means for saving the lost. When people are eliminated from the missions thrust, ill directed and misguided technology takes the driver's seat.

A church is not a missions minded church when people are encouraged to remain at home rather than encouraged to go to the dark corners of the world. A church is not a missions minded church when it skimps on mission giving in order to meet its home expenses.

Fear that too many faithful supporters will leave the church for the mission field, thereby plunging the church into a financial strait, is unfounded. This attitude is unscriptural and proven false by experience. Any church that suffers because too many leave for the mission field needs to close. Any church that gives so much to effective mission work that it can not meet its home operating expenses, should trim its home budget.

One pastor of a church in a small Northwestern town, ready to build a new building for an expanding church, decided to have a missions conference first. The church gave $24,000 to missions in that week, a staggering sum for a young church less than two years old. It did not slow the provision of the new building. Instead, of slowing its membership growth or delaying the much needed building, the church paid in full for the new building within one year and the membership continues to grow. The membership of 100 sacrificially gave to missions and God honored that giving by doubling the membership.

Another pastor with a membership of less than a hundred, in the midst of building a new building in order to get out of cramped quarters, watched as two of his most faithful tithers went to China as missionaries. What happened to the church? Within 3 years it moved into a new facility which is fully paid for. Souls are being saved. Others joined the church and attendance has increased.

Another church with a membership of over seven hundred is amazing. No traveling gospel quartets (dis)grace its podium. On each Saturday evening, a group of two hundred men meet for prayer for two hours. In any church service one can see that this is a church of families--with husbands and fathers leading the way. The church's foreign missions budget exceeds one million dollars a year. The church needed more room for services. Folding chairs are used in every service. Instead of allocating mission funds into a "home missions project" for a new auditorium, in addition to its regular support,the church gave $180,000 in one week to a group of missionaries. Several families from the church are on the foreign field. One of the assistant pastors is leaving to start a new church in a small mountain town. The church committed themselves to supporting him financially for one year. The church supports those who go out from the church to the foreign mission field with one-half of their needed support. This is in addition to an annual amount of $600,000 given to missonaries out of other churches. The church is located in the midst of "Mormon country" in a small city.

A pastor and wife in a small town of East Tennessee works and supports their family of seven-and have done so for over fifteen years. They receive only token ministry expenses from the church and personally give back many times more than they receive. The church supports twenty missionaries and does more than a thousand churches ten times its size. The pastor has been to several countries on mission trips and is a valuable part of a worldwide missions group that establishes churches in remote areas and closed countries. There are no entertainment packages or social programs or seminars. Services are straight forward preaching and teaching of the Word.

CONSIDER WHAT I SAY AND THE LORD WILL

Some who fail to see the import of world evangelism and the responsibility of the church to do it, do so because there is an almost universal failure in the church to make a difference between the Lord's *earthly* preaching and His *heavenly* preaching. For the most part, churches try to pattern their work after the revelation in Matthew, Mark, Luke and John, and fail to see the distinctive revelation of God's program for this present age as revealed by Jesus Christ through Paul, the apostle to the Gentiles. This neglect brought about a mission's effort that is crippled at the beginning.

A zealous devotional approach to the word of God will produce a flurry of enviable activity. But, sooner or later, that zeal must be tempered by sound doctrine. If it is not, frustration, defeat, or unsound doctrines take control. This is true in an individual's life and it is proven in church history.

After the cross and just before the Lord returned back to heaven, He gathered His church together and told them to go and tell the world of His kingdom with the added promise that He would return and set up his kingdom on earth.

Peter and that early church did not know the full benefits of the Lord's substitutionary work at calvary. To them, the resurrection was the most powerful event. They are "witnesses of his resurrection from the dead." The meaning of the cross is to them that method used by the Romans to carry out the wishes of Israel's leaders to be rid of the "King of the Jews." He came proclaiming the good news of the kingdom of heaven. He met all the prophetic demands of that King who would rule over Israel on the throne of David (II Samuel 7). "He came unto his own and his own received him not."(John 1:12). The apostles under Peter's leadership taught "Did not His resurrection proved that He was Who He said He was?" The Holy Ghost is sent upon them to become witnesses of the coming King, who will make His enemies His footstool. They are to begin in Jerusalem but extending to the uttermost parts of the world. (Acts 1:8)

Paul is saved in Acts 9 and the Lord appears to him on several occasions. the purpose of these appearances is to give to Paul, the apostle of the Gentiles, the revelation of the gospel of the grace of God so that all the world may know the completed salvation offered to all peoples.
"God hath given to us the ministry of reconciliation, to wit, that God was in Christ reconciling the world unto himself"

The average church in the USA is probably so far gone, there is no recourse. There is hope for those who are going out to begin a new church and ministry. A church can keep its original purpose and even grow with a mission's ministry. It dos not have to turn a blind eye and deaf ear to world evangelization. If this book does anything to change the course of a few pastors, or students, or churches, it will have served its purpose.

I. THE BEGINNING AND REASON FOR THE EXISTENCE OF THE LOCAL CHURCH.

The reason the local church exists at all is because of missions. Someone brought the gospel to the shores of the country and established a local church. In its early years, to some degree that church continued to carry the gospel to other parts of the home country and other churches were established.

This is perhaps oversimplification but it is essentially what happens. Someone said "God's own Son was a missionary when He left heaven's glory and came to earth to save men." This is true. Churches are not products of some spontaneous spiritual combustion. No church starts on its own. There is always someone who is burdened to tell others about Jesus Christ at its very foundation.

The substitutionary work of Jesus Christ for a lost world demands our substitutionary work on His behalf to tell what He did. Reaching out to others is the very heart of God. The person who follows God will do the same. The problem is, we get so involved with day by day existence *where we are* we lose sight of the bigger picture and how we relate to it.

No sincere person means to ignore missions. To do so is to deny his own experience when he was saved. Another person came and told him about Jesus. If no one goes, no one hears. But as with all matters of religion, the "little foxes spoil the vines" and creep into theology and its practice to reduce it to baser things.

SOME DEFINITIONS

A definition of "Foreign Missions."
"Church evangelism which requires selectively trained fulltime personel that extends beyond the church's local culture,boundaries and usual scope of activity."

Foreign missions involves several distincive elements:
1. Selected personel.
2. Specially trained personel.
3. Fulltime personel.
4. Personel who minister outside the ability of the local church's normal activities.
5. Personel who live and minister in a foreign culture outside the local churches' ability to reach on a regular basis.

A definition of "Home Missions."

"Church evangelism by a selective, trained group which reaches out to those not normally included within the resposibility of local church evangelistic endeavors, and who live within the local church's home country."

Home missions involves several distinctive elements:
1. Selected personel.
2. Specially trained personel.
3. Fulltime personel.
4. Personel who live within the continental USA.
5. Personel who minister to those outside the local churches' ability to reach.

From the above definitions we see that Foreign and Home missions are quite similar, with a few distinctive differences.

Home missions is fulltime evangelism by a selective, trained group to others who are outside the church's own culture,or language, or physical proximity. Sunday School, Bible school, Youth camps,Bible camps,Camp meetings,bus ministries,radio broadcasts,Christian schools, athletic outreaches do not meet this definition. All of these activities fall under the normal responsibilities of the local church.

Home missions requires a person who is prepared and appointed. Some examples of home missions are: Exclusive fulltime American Indian ministries, Exclusive Hispanic ministries, Exclusive fulltime prison ministries. Home missions is an exclusive fulltime ministry to those who live within the local church's country but who are denied normal access to the gospel by language, or culture, or law.

Confusion is brought about by mixing Christian school, camp or bus ministries with foreign missions or home missions. A lack of clear distinction between foreign and home missions can also obscure the church's vision and effectiveness. Without a clear definition and recognition of the church's responsibility toward world evangelism, the resulting denial hurts the cause of missions in general.

The common practice of finding one in the USA who has never heard a clear presentation of the gospel, and using that instance to reduce the need to get the gospel to those millions who have never heard in a foreign land, is one example of confusing mission responsibility. or-estab jail, nursing home, sports witness- in order to involve people and resources in a "close" ministry.).
Average concept of missions-the field-duties-culture-
Real picture
I. The need for Foreign missions
    A. Scripture commands
    B. Distribution of workers
    C. World and field conditions
    D. The American potential

II. 21st Century missions-a new look at an old task
lets get thhe job done!
    A. Technology
        1. Travel
        2. Communications
            a. Telephone
            b. Fax
            c. Computer
            d. Ham radio
            e. Publications
        3. Support organizations
    B. Traditional vs. Innovative Missions

1. Transplanted American Church vs. Indigenous
2. Deskbound vs. Interactive Mission Board
3. Independent vs. Interdependent
4. Deputation vs. Pre-Field Ministry
5. Indefinite vs. Definitive Missions
6. Raising Money vs. Support Building
7. Long Term vs. Short Term Missionaries
8. Mission Conferences vs. Mission Churches
9. Fixed Role Missionaries vs. Flexible Missionaries
10.

C. Financial Support of Missions.
1. Faith promise
2, Grace giving principle
3. Special projects
4. Tithing

CRITICISM IN CHINA

The word involves a broad spectrum in China. Under Chairman Mao's rules it may cover self-confession of faults to the neighborhood or work unit. It can also mean a complaint lodged about service received or given. We recently took a required tour to a local site in Guizhou Province. The tour was in connection with an education conference. My purpose was to be accredited so that we could place missionaries as English teachers. The day long trip covered a visit to a bridge, minority village, the largest waterfall in Asia and a meal in a minority operated restaurant.

Tours are interesting to say the least. Any "tour" in China is coupled with unexpected surprises. One can expect to be treated to unstated stops along the way. Our tour had a stop at a crystal factory and a tea shop in addition to the scheduled ones. The tour operators strike up deals with various businesses, hopeful of gathering the riches of the foreigners and Chinese vacationers.

The crystal factory is actually a store outlet of the factory where various crystal pieces are sold as well as "junk": items such as sunglasses, cigarettes, lighters, paper mache, all of which have nothing to do with crystals. The minority restaurant furnished the basis of "criticism." On the tour advertisement, a promise was made:
Meal at Minority Restaurant.

Ethnic food with Eight Courses. (Actually, we had rice, green vegetable, chicken with mushrooms and smoked pork with garlic shoots. This added up to 5 courses if you count the drink.)

After the unscheduled stop at the crystal factory and the promised restaurant, we went to the "famous" bridge. This bridge is not a bridge at all. It is about one hundred stones set in 3 feet of water that winds through a small walk between a group of rocks.

Around each bend of the walk there is a merchant selling the same trinkets as all others. Various minority girls are also positioned along the way who try to persuade each visitor to take a picture with them. Prices to pose with the girls range from $2 to $4 US, all depending upon the elaborateness of the girl's dresses.

The "largest waterfall in Asia" is also coupled with the longest walk in Asia. At least one mile down a steep path provides all the tourists with great training for mountain climbing. On the way back to the hotel, we stopped at a tea shop and were treated to a sales pitch of their various teas, all available for a price.

When we returned to the hotel, the Chinese education people announced they were going to meet with the tour owner and "criticize" him for the poor service on the tour. "Great idea," I said, thinking of the long walk to the falls, the incessant nagging to buy goods, or even the "air-conditioned bus" in which the only AC was the open window.

We were surprised that the criticism was set for 9 PM that night at the education leader's hotel room. I was also surprised that none of my concerns were on the agenda. The Chinese participants were going to criticize the tour company for the 3 courses lacking in the "eight course meal." To top it off, the tour company owner was to show up at the hotel at 9 PM to receive his criticism. Show up he did, and the official complaint was lodged with great fanfare about the lacking dishes at the meal. The owner answered with gushing apologies and promised to mend his ways in the future.

I was somewhat shocked at the trivial (in my eyes) complaint, as well as the owner coming to the hotel at 9 PM to receive his dressing down. However, in China, the presentation of a meal is much more important than anything else. Promise an air conditioned bus but only provide a cart—call a line of stones a bridge—or have folks sweat for an hour on a mountain walk—but never, ever, promise an eight course meal and only provide 5 courses!

MANY CHOICES WHEN EATING OUT IN THE USA

"Good evening," the maitre d' said. "Table for four?"
"Yes. Thank you."

"Smoking or non?"
"Nonsmoking."

"Would you prefer to dine indoors or outdoors this evening?"
"I guess indoors would be good."

"Very well, sir," he said. "Would you like to be seated in the main
dining room, the enclosed patio, or our lovely solarium?"
"Uh, let me see … uh …"
"I can give you a table with a lovely view in out lovely solarium."
"I think the solarium would be lovely," I said. We followed him
there.

"Now, would you prefer a view overlooking the golf course, the
sunset on
the lake or the majestic mountains to the west?"
"Whatever you recommend," I said. *Let him make a decision for a
change, I
thought.* He sat us by a window facing the golf course, the lake or
the
mountains. I couldn't tell which because it was dark outside.

Then a young man better dressed and better looking than any of us
presented himself at our table. "Good evening, my name is Paul,
and I'll be your
waiter this evening.
Would you like a few minutes before I take your order?"

"No," I said. "I'm just a meat-and-potatoes guy, so I'll have the steak and a baked potato."
"12 oz or 16 oz?"
"12 oz."
"Soup or salad?"
"Salad."

"We have a mixed-green salad, hearts of palm or a very fine endive salad
with baby shrimp."
"Just a mixed-green salad, okay?"

"Whatever you say sir. Dressing?"
I didn't want to make another decision. "Whatever you've got will be
fine."

"We have creamy Italian, blue cheese, vinigrette, Thousand Island, honey
Dijon, ranch…."
"Just bring me one. Surprise me."

"Creamy Italian is our house specialty. Would that be all right, sir?"
"Yeah." I was curt. I was done with civility.

"And your baked potato…"
I knew what was coming, "I just want the baked potato dry, you understand? I don't want anything on it."

"No butter? No sour cream?"
"No."

"No chives?"

"No! Don't you understand English?" I shouted. "I don't want anything on
it.
Just bring me a baked potato and a steak."

"Would you prefer the six-, eight- or 12-ounce steak, sir?"
"Whatever."

"Would you like that rare, medium rare, medium, medium well or well done?
Or, if you prefer, we can butterfly it for you."

"Pauly Boy," I said, "you are really starting to get me steamed."
"Which brings up the vegetables, sir, Would you like steamed broccoli,
creamed corn, sauteed zucchini, diced carrots--"

That did it. I threw my napkin to the floor, stood up, put my face right
In his arrogant kisser and said, "How'd you like to settle this outside?"
"Fine with me, sir. Would you prefer the parking lot, the side alley or
the street in front of the restaurant?"

"I prefer right here," I said, and sucker-punched him. He ducked, then
countered with a left hook right under my eye. It was the first time all
night he hadn't offered me a selection. I collapsed semiconscious into my
chair, as someone in authority rushed over and berated Pauly. I felt my tie being

loosened, my collar unbuttoned, hands slapping my face. When I regained
my senses, I saw the very concerned maitre d' right in front of my nose. He
apologized and offered to buy me a drink, call
the paramedics--whatever I wanted.

"No, no," I said. "I'll be all right. Just bring me a glass of water."
"Yes, sir, right away," he said. "Would you prefer imported mineral water, sparkling water or club soda with a wedge of lime?"---
Anonymous author

HONEST EVALUATION OF DISHONEST FILIPINO PREACHERS

Extreme poverty can make a crook out of a normally honest man. Human nature apart from following the word of God is corrupt—in all cultures! For example, there is one Filipino student pastor named JM who chose not to follow our Filipino leadership. Like some, he would get addresses from people who visit us in the Philippines and then send a pitiful or 'spiritual' prayer request to the USA gullible ears for money. Then they receive US dollars from various places and are accountable to no one.

JM inflated the results of an incomplete medical exam a couple of years ago to the effect that he had cancer of the lymph system. He supposedly needed $2500 USD for treatment. He sent it to my home church, without telling anybody he had done so—including his Filipino pastor (Brother F) who was taking up an offering for him to pay for his medicine. Suspecting a rat, I got the report along with blood tests, and sent it to a couple of USA medical folks who concurred he simply had an infection and no cancer. We were right. It has been about 2 years now and JM hasn't missed a lick.

A well meaning individual (thinking he would save Jimmy's life) almost sent $2500 for Jimmy to blow on himself. He still got letters off to others and collected hundreds of dollars. Later he was the talk of the village as he rode around in his new clothes on his $300 bike, and healthy as a horse. During this whole time he was playing basketball each day for 2-3 hours-I told him he was the wellest sick person I had ever seen.

JM is still at it after being dismissed from Bible school. He is a smooth talker but has no ministry our Filipino leadership would approve.

He is a single, immature, can't preach, a Bible school get-by student, who sports flashy sunglasses, name brand clothes, a new bike worth $300 and lives with his mother. When our Filipino pastoral board rejected his "mission" call to a tourist island (this is the topless beach European packed playground of the PI), he redirected his efforts, now claiming to have a "Bible study" started and still writing "prayer letters" and praising God for the USD.

We recently sacked one man, TB, because he wasn't doing anything, and put his support to one who was in the jungle doing a work for God. Some saved men are too lazy to work and too independent to follow, but parasitic enough to hang around those who are doing something.

Seeing and knowing these things, I can understand why some wiser pastors refuse to support nationals altogether--it is foolish to throw God's money away on the basis of a letter from some unknown who is a novice and refuses trained leadership.

$50 is small change in the USA. But in the PI where a good job pays $50 a month, some irresponsible, lazy nationals pull the wool over the eyes of USA churches. Kodak pictures can be and are staged. Wiser than a serpent, they quickly learn the "church language" and praise the Lord while they bilk funds out of beguiled USA folks. I could take you to 100 places where this is going on and has gone on for years in the PI.

If they do get an American visitor, they prepare and know how to make it look spiritual and pitiful when he comes for his five-day run and gun visit. Filipino con men in church work are plentiful like everywhere else; they chuckle over the gullible Americans and easy money.

A wise pastor would never send money to an unknown in the USA on the basis of a letter only-no matter what it said or claimed. Why do it because it has an overseas stamp on it?

That is not missions, it is sheer stupidity. For every handwritten letter you receive from a national, you can be sure at least 25 other people in the USA got the same handwritten letter!

Anyone who wants to come and see our work can--it will not be setup overnight for you-you can't set this up overnight-we'll take you to Mindanao and let you see a church of over 200 in the middle of the jungle. We'll take you on a mountain path 5 miles further to see our graduate pastoring 50 people with hardly any clothes, we'll let you see the 5 new churches, and 14 others, we'll let you see 42 resident Bible school students faithfully training--and we'll let you meet our Filipino pastors who lead the work. I'll furnish you with my references of men who have known me for over 25 years and know my "track" record. We'll show you where the support is going and how much of it goes where. That is the proper responsibility of a missionary. Talk is cheap but the proof is in the pudding. 15 mature, experienced USA pastors and 10 medical professionals have seen this work with their own eyes during the past five years and can testify to these things.

At the same time there are many Filipino brethren in other organizations who are doing a good work and winning souls and we praise the Lord for them.

CULTURAL DIFFERENCES AMID SMILES, SIRS AND LAUGHTER

Everyone is smiling and politely greeting you: "Good morning, sir." "Good morning, ma'am." The only problem is that amidst the smiles and sirs you are getting nothing done and the important things are ignored. You get the smiles and sirs and flowers and complimentary fruit at a local hotel, but you can't get water to brush your teeth.

You are sitting in a Philippine restaurant. One person asks what you would like to drink. Another person shows up and asks the same question, "What would you like to drink?" About 5 minutes later, a third person brings you your drink. You wonder why the initial person who asked you what you wanted to drink did not tell the person who brings the drinks. One trip is made to your table to rearrange the plates. Another trip is made to rearrange the silverware. You wonder why two trips were made when one could have done it all in good time.

Asian culture through our Western eyes is bumfuzzling! We are so concerned with time and efficiency, the relationship oriented Asian seems to be inefficient and ignorant. After 8 years we are still amazed at the cultural differences between East and West.

Starving for some kind of Western environment and food, you head for Pizza Hut when you go through Manila. Just like home! --well, you had better wait before you get too excited. The Pizza Hut in Harrison Plaza in Manila boasts on the menu that your lunch pizza will be delivered to your table in 12 minutes, or your next pizza is free. Really? No. You see, if the restaurant is busy, all the waiter does is explain that *your pizza* will take a little longer. This personal explanation negates written promises.

A Bible school graduate stands to give his testimony. He is overwhelmed and begins to cry, unable to speak. All the congregation begin to laugh and talk among themselves. I have a motorcycle wreck in the mountains, possibly breaking my leg. The villagers all begin to laugh!

The Westerner's reaction in either case is one of shock or disgust. Actually, in both cases the Filipinos are sorry that such misfortune occured and are trying by laughter to alleviate the discomfort.

A person dies. The body is kept at the home for several days and people who visit play cards, gamble, sing songs, gossip, eat, and generally have a rip-roaring good time. The Westerner is really pained at the callousness and uncaring attitudes when actually, the opposite is true. This activity is an effort to ease the pain.

We think the Eastern culture is ridiculous but are unable to see our cultural inconsistencies. We have the Western custom of bringing food to a deceased persons home after the funeral and think nothing of it. We criticize the Asian for bringing fruit to a graveside. When asked "When is your dead loved one going to eat fruit?" the Asian replied, "At the same time your dead loved one smells the flowers."

PRACTICAL WORK AND COMMON SENSE

During a recent ecumenical gathering, someone rushed in shouting, "The building is on fire!"

The Methodists gathered in the corner and prayed.
The Baptists cried, "Where is the water?"
The Brethren began a Bible study on "Fire".
Benny Hinn was severely burned trying to lay hands on the fire.
The Quakers quietly praised God for the blessings that fire brings.
The Lutherans posted a notice on the door declaring that fire was evil.
The Romans Catholics organized a Bingo party to raise funds to cover the damage.
The Charismatics called Toronto to check the most recent revelations on fire.
The Jews placed symbols on the door post and lintels hoping that the fire would pass over them.
Oral Roberts had a vision of a 100 ft. fire truck.
The Congregationalists shouted, "Every person for himself."
The Fundamentalist proclaimed, "It is the vengeance of God."
The Christian Scientists agreed among themselves that there was not a fire.
The Presbyterians appointed a chairperson who was to appoint a committee to look into the matter and make a written report to the session.
The Episcopalians formed a procession and marched out.

And the secretary grabbed a fire extinguisher and put the fire out!

RADIO BROADCASTS

The radio broadcasts are going fine. I'm having to wrestle with the station on the scheduling--we get 15 minute broadcasts taped and they give us 30 min-I said, "Just put two messages on back to back!" I put 12 broadcasts on Romans-simple salvation, challenge type messages.

Brother T put two months worth on tape and they are airing them now. He is a good preacher and sound as they come. His church (one of our outreaches we started), New Testament. Baptist, runs about 150 in attendance and he has folks saved and baptized regularly. Although he graduated from Doane Bible college several years ago, he wanted to get the KJB issue and more doctrine so he attended our night classes for two years while he was pastoring and being Dean of Men in our resident school. He is also one of our Filipino Field Committee members along with Pastors F, B and L. I am impressed with his ability, dedication, and love for the Book, so he was a natural choice to be one of our radio preachers. In fact, all of the above men preach on the radio in addition to myself.

We are getting the Negros (Island, not race!) broadcast at a good rate, about $150 a month, so we are going to put on another broadcast on an Iloilo station. We think the radio had to do with one of our new students who came last week to enroll in our night school.

PROPERTY

Everything here, except time, moves as slow as molasses in Montana. And, I'm always discovering new situations. One recent one is the fact that one section of our property (where the school buildings are located-about 3 acres) which was bought in about 1986 never got the title transferred into Calvary Baptist's name. The original owner's (who since died) present heirs own it -technically- although we have record of payment.

As you can imagine, I think it is a priority to get the legal stuff up to date. The heirs are friendly toward us, so no problem there. I began last fall, when I was aware of the title deal, to get Pastor F to start legal work with a lawyer, and all that stuff. Well, long story shortened, this past week Bro. F told me--it took 6 months to get this info--the lawyer had finally talked to the heirs and they are ready to do the title change.

However, --here it comes--as always--they own other property and they have not paid taxes on any of it for ten years. I said, "Well we should pay the taxes for the property we are on, since we have used it and they should pay for the other." Honest, fair and simple, right? Wrong! The reply was, "Well the people are afraid they will have to pay all their taxes, 52,000 pesos for the past 10 years, if they bring the school property to the tax collector's attention, and, they have no money.

So, another typical cultural "problem." They are quite willing to transfer the title, by this they meet the acceptable standard of conduct--however they "have no money" to pay taxes on all their property --this culturally excuses them from obligation---therefore, the only way to get the property title changed is for -you know who-to pay their tax bill for them! No amount of our logic or reasoning works in these situations. Stuff like this happens all the time. It's a puzzle to us how they can excuse themselves on such issues by this type of maneuver, but I guess we do the same ourselves in some areas but, dadburn, life does get "tegious."

MEDICAL

We all understand you can't teach the Bible to dead students-so mission work in remote areas make a doctor of some sorts of us all.

I'm up to my neck in medical stuff and I think I might make a MD yet..heh! heh! heh!.... We've got about 8 students with sore throats, congestion, tonsils swollen and red, some fever, coughing, deep stuff...so without a stethoscope (I need to learn how to use one of those things) or anybody else...(my partner in crime, uh, medical practice, Sue, is way over in NH with Catherine nursing sick kids at Bible camp for five weeks)....but with Don Harris's donated nurses drug handbook for dosages, and Stephen Reese's books on drugs-- plus past exp., I decided to give them amoxicillin (no choice-our med supplies are low-it was either that or J&J baby powder) for the respiratory infection, pseudoval for the sinus drainage, and tylenol for the aches. If I had a horseshoe I'd given that too, for good luck!

Emanuel got his first treatment of sulfadiazine on his erupted lymph nodes yesterday afternoon that Don Harris sent me. The prior 15 days of bactroban and daily cleaning by one of our ladies here really worked. His sores look 100% better-- most of the neck is cleared but scarred over and his chest sores are reduced to about 1/4" X 3". I jokingly told him his sores had healed better than my moth attack. 3 weeks ago I had to show him moth sores on my chest before he would take off his shirt and let me treat his sores-I have since wondered if the Lord let that moth get on me and dump those sores so I could eventually treat Emanuel. If so, I'm glad Emanuel hadn't been crushed by a carabao..........

Serious question about Emanuel--understanding that "lymph node" eruption was what he told me and that someone could have told him that back in the jungle who knew less than I know about medicine--I noticed this looks like it has happened before-there are older scars where similar occurrences seemed to have taken place-are we seeing a possibility of TB of the skin?

TB is common in the PI. For example one of our new Bible school students who had seen a doctor in Mindanao and was diagnosed with active TB came to me yesterday late to let me know after being here almost 4 weeks in the crowded dorm with other students. He was out of whatever medicine he was supposed to take, had lost the prescript, didn't know the name of it, etc.--seeing this happen before in the PI and knowing he has no money at all---what probably happened was that he went to a regional charity hospital for a TB test-was identified as positive and given a prescription but he promptly threw it away, not having money to buy it.

We do have one Bible student man 22 years old with a lump the size of a large black eye pea in the center of his neck about 1" above the v of the collarbone and below the "adams apple" when his head is extended. The lump is moveable and not connected to anything underneath as far as I can tell. There is no opening on the surface-it is not red, hot to the touch or painful. He is from the jungle in Mindanao and I'm the first "doctor (!)" he has ever seen. He said the lump had been there 5 years. IF-IF-IF, our communication was good, I understand the size has not changed for a year. There are no external problems apparent with his skin in that area or thers. I told him not to worry about it right now. He does come from an inland area with a no seafood. His diet is almost strictly corn and meat with little iodized salt and from where neck goiters are common, especially among older women. I've seen it. But is doesn't look anything like a goiter to me. It is more cyst-like in appearance but in a strange place at the V of his neck.

What we need in medicine: plastic gloves, vitamins for adults and children, 4X4 gauze pads, tape, antibiotics such as erythr, amox, pen VK, ibuprofen, tylenol, pseudoval, any antihistamines, anti fungal creams, BACTROBAN works miracles on skin sores!!! , plus anything else anyone can send--what we can't use or don't know how to use, we donate to a country hospital to "swap out" for services such as the TB tests I'm sending our "TB" man to this morning. Then we'll buy his prescriptions for him. No narcotics, legend drugs can be shipped but anything else can.

SPIRITUAL SIDE OF THINGS:

We have 42 Bible students (one got homesick and played a John Mark on us) in resident school, all training to go back to their villages or other remote areas to start Baptist churches. We have 28 more in night school, learning more Bible who are already in full time work. They ride their bicycles, tricycles (PI taxis) or jeeps to get here and back on Monday and Tuesday evenings.

I taught the Book of Ruth for 1 1/2 hours and Bible Doctrine on faith 1 !/2 hours last night to our night school. All power went out at 3PM and stayed out all night, and is still out at 7AM this morning. The class was held outside under a full moon and I used my flashlight to read my Bible and put things on a blackboard. Slinging sweat and breathing fire. When the mosquitoes started eating, we had to move into the hotter, darker, inside classroom where the screens kept tormenters at bay. So, I did what I've done many times over the years, taught the Bible in the dark. Where in the USA can you get 30 people who have worked all day to sit in a hot 95 degree 100% humid dark room with one flashlight and study the Bible for 3 hours--and not one complaint? Not many.

Some of our 20-25 year old resident students are wearing shoes for the first time in their life. We got them the best we had on hand and it sure is funny to watch them shuffle around in them.

We have 44 pastors and staff members whom we support each month in entirety. That's a bill of about $3,000 US---God provides each month--we trust Him by faith to send it in and He has!

Our food bill for our resident Bible school students 42 X $20 per month is $840. God provided that with special offerings this month.

We literally live by faith each month from His hand. I'm convinced that if we do what we can do, God meets the needs. Lack of necessities come about when we put ourselves where God did not lead. I used to read about George Mueller and miraculous events with needs being met--we're no George Mueller by any stretch of the imagination, but bless God, the same Lord who provided for him, provides for any of His children. And, if material goods we think should come, doesn't, He has a lesson for us in it, and we still receive what we need. Where He guides, He thoroughly provides.

5 new churches were started in the past 12 months where no churches existed before in the areas. Now there are 19 churches we see God supplying the needs for. Over 300 are saved and baptized each month. Responsible, trained Filipinos we trained and know lead these churches --and they follow our Filipino leadership.

Besides this, we are building, by faith, two buildings here at Calvary and have 6 more in progress around the islands.

When I think of my wish list---We need $100,000 to build purchase new property, build two new dorms to replace our two that are literally falling down-and man, would it be nice to just have somebody with it sitting in the bank, to do something with it that would count for eternity! Right now, we're limited in training Filipinos only by space--we've got every dorm packed and some of our floors propped up to keep them from collapsing.

If we had a lawn mower and weed eater our students would not have to cut grass with a machete.--and boy, do we have grass!

If we had a medical professional MD or RN to leave the padded life and set up a missionary med clinic, what a blessing that would be.

My untrained hands are mighty rough on touchy cuts and infections, the Filipinos are praying for gentler hands. My wife is preferred over me. She talks, soothes feelings, and has the training--I just poke and scrape.

The key to reaching the Philippines is to train Filipinos. One properly trained, responsible Filipino is worth more than 10 western missionaries. For the money it takes for one American to finally get trained and stay on the field, we can train 100 Filipinos and do 1,000 times more within five years.

Eating rice instead of Burger King's and taking GI showers (our wells are dry now) and scratching bug bites, killing rats, ants, snakes, running down roaches that can read and write, itching from the incessant heat, etc., gets the best of many of our delicate American brethren. Our Filipino brethren see it as "the normal Christian Life."

Some have asked what is the best way to support our PI work. The best way is to put us on a regular prayer list and call our name and work out to the Lord each day. If you wish to send monetary support, you may designate it or undesignate it.

All designated funds go 100% as you direct. The undesignated are put into the PI needs as our field committee directs. Every cent is tax deductible when made out to EOTEM and sent to our EOTEM financial office in the USA. IRS does not recognize offerings made payable to a foreign church or individual. Our financial office is self-funded (something else the Lord provided) so your entire offering goes to the field.
Make the check to: "EOTEM" and mark on the lower left "Reese-PI", send a note with it if you wish it to go to a particular project. Mail to:
EOTEM
PO BOX 4574
Beeville Texas 78104

You will receive a receipt at the end of the month and a prayer letter report from me as well.

"And the things that thou hast heard of me among many witnesses, the same commit thou to faithful men, who shall be able to teach others also."
(II Timothy 2:2 KJB)
Dr. Dave Reese

REMOTE MISSIONARY WORK IN MEXICO

The story begins with a retired railroad engineer hearing my husband teach a Bible lesson. He realized he was lost and accepted Christ. His wife Karen was reared a Catholic and was saved soon after. Roger enrolled in our Bible school, visited Mexico, saw the needs, and he and his wife went to Mexico as missionaries. They labored for over 30 years to carry the gospel to Mexico.

Andrea lies quietly on the bed under a clean, warm, fleece blanket in an old adobe shack. This is the bed she has slept on for most of her 86 years.
A large tumor crowds her lungs and throat. It is evident her time is short. Reaching to me, I feel the feverish hand clasp mine in a loving hold, one that welcomes and speaks much more than a hello. Her dark eyes affirm the same welcome message. This little grandmother is curled on the bed, waiting—waiting for her Jesus to take her to Heaven. "He takes too long to come," she says in a whispered tone.

Back when Andrea could walk, she had gone to the little deserted church building. Every day for over a year, she wept and prayed. Every prayer was a plea for God to send someone to her rancho to tell them about Him. Many days passed and God answered her prayer.

God worked in the hearts of Roger and Karen Bowman to go to Mexico. They believed God wanted them to work in the rural, out-of-the-way places. The ranchos where missionaries are scarce were their targets. Hunting a rancho in which to begin, Roger and Karen drove over the wild, rugged, back country outside the city of Saltillo. They passed two ranchos and came to the one where the grandmother had prayed for someone to come.

Roger began a Bible study and Karen taught the children, using flannelgraph stories. Soon 5 adults and 5 children were saved. Recently, Dave and I visited the work in Mexico. The village people prepared us a meal of goat stew, bean soup, and tortillas-"from scratch." Afterwards, we held a service. Dave preached and Roger translated into Spanish.

As I sat listening to Roger translate the message, I thought of the little grandmother in her adobe house. When Jesus does come to take her to Heaven, wouldn't you like to see this Mexican grandmother as she enters Heaven's gates? "In my father's house are many mansions"...and one belongs to this grandmother who prayed for her rancho to hear about Jesus.
Roger and Karen Bowman are the missionaries God sent to these fields "white unto harvest." They were obedient to His command to GO.

Others in this world are waiting to hear. Many Christians refuse to go and tell the good news of salvation. Our debt is coming due, and it is not paid!
"I am debtor both to the Greeks, and to the Barbarians..."
(Romans 1:14 KJB)
"So then every one of us shall give account of himself to God."(
Romans 14:12 KJB)
--Sue Reese

CHINA: FIRST AND LASTING IMPRESSIONS

This article is written by one of my brothers. Roger is saved, has a definite part in our mission work, and was Vice President of a prestigious Chicago bank when he took this trip to China with us.

When my brother asked me to go to China with him and his wife in February of this year (1994), I was somewhat apprehensive but yet excited about the opportunity. After all, this would be my first journey outside of North America. As one with a business background, I was going to lend his journey a sense of credibility (at least in the eyes of the government of China). As well, we were extremely interested in establishing a business presence there since the country does not have freedom of religion and one must appear to be something other than a pastor. As I began planning for the trip, the early realization that China is not an open country hit me when I found that one must obtain a Visa for travel there, not only explaining my travel's purpose but also where I was to stay and when I was to return. But without too much trouble, I was soon on my way not really believing how easy it was to get on an airplane and soon be 10,000 miles from home entering China through immigration and customs.

Landing at Beijing airport some 40 hours later left me with my first "culture shock". Even though I am certain that many others had taken the same steps which I took, I could not help but feel an uneasiness since I was only one of a few Caucasians in a sea of Orientals. When I finally exited customs some 60 minutes after landing, one can not imagine the relief when I saw my brother and an in-country missionary waiting for me. The city of Beijing is dirty and there are vast numbers of people and bicycles everywhere. One thing became very clear. There is no shortage of manpower and it appears that where they lack technology, they can and do make up for it with lots of workers.

After settling into the hotel, which by the way compared very well to any American hotel, our first business meeting took place. China has a great desire for anything American and is thirsting for large investments to make their infrastructure more efficient. This was abundantly clear in the several meetings we had while in China. And from a business perspective, there appeared to be a great deal of opportunity. However, the business climate there is best described as immature and largely uneducated, at least in American methods. This was our biggest obstacle.

For example, in our review of approximately 15 investment projects, not one person handed us anything in writing or had any pictures or other presentation material to help us understand not only the need but just exactly what they were talking about. Of course, all communication took place through translators which, in and of itself, is difficult even when both parties clearly understand what is being said. We did obtain one brochure from a milk production factory but it had more grammatical mistakes than anything I have ever seen produced in this country, even by 10 or 12 year old students. One thing which kept us laughing was this dairy company's logo, which turned out to be a bull.

While in Beijing, we received word that a missionary in a nearby city had been visited by the police and there was a real concern about what might happen to him and his family. Since my brother had met this person, I had my first sense of uneasiness over how easily the government might be able to connect us to him. If they were able to establish a connection, I had no idea what might happen to us. At the least, our trip would surely be cut short and we would be summarily told to leave.

Our commitments also took us to a large city of several million in Northeast China and there we continued to review projects amid a city and population which, at best, can be described as backward.

By American standards their cleanliness would not pass even the lowest level of acceptance. The habit of spitting on floors, never cleaning carpets and filthy restaurants with torn and soiled tablecloths were things that faced me on this first venture to Asia.

One thing was obvious however. If a person even appears to have any money for investments, they will be warmly received. Upon arrival, we were met by a dozen or so government officials at the airport at 10:00 at night! They drove us to a hotel which was not the one we were expecting explaining that the other one required a deposit and they did not think we would be willing to pay it. This was the first of many instances of our manipulation by these otherwise friendly people. The hotel staff did not contain one person who could speak or understand English. But the government delegation through our assigned translator did a good job of getting us checked in and the delegation actually took our luggage to our rooms for us.

After settling in, I thought it would be a good time to call my office to see how things were going (about 10:00 A.M. there) only to find that the modern looking telephone would not work. All I got was a strange signal. I called the hotel operator only to be greeted with this voice in Chinese who could not understand a word I said so she merely hung up. Somewhat frustrated, I went down to the hotel front desk only to find it deserted but I did find three security people guarding an empty lobby. After several minutes of hand gestures, I finally got the message across. I wanted to make a phone call! They found a somewhat sleepy clerk who again could not understand my request so back I went to try again.

After 2 hours, I finally got through to the office. All the while this was happening, a sense of helplessness and concern was growing, especially given what we had been told about the missionary while we were in Beijing.

Here I was in a Communist country, sitting in a city where no one (except the American missionary and he had gone home) could speak my language, placed in a hotel selected by Government officials and, on top of all that, telephones did not function even though they were a part of a very modern system. It was clear that we were at the mercy of our hosts.

After making connection, I did not know when I would next be able to talk to my office so I instructed them to do whatever is necessary to find me if they had not heard from me within the next four days. In other words, I told them to call out the dogs and track me down starting with the American embassy in Beijing. Fortunately, things did work out and I was able to leave one very short cryptic message with the answering service the next day that we were okay before my phone call was cut off. For the next 48 hours, my phone was inoperable. I don't know for sure but I have a nagging belief that the phone did not work on purpose. Today, I believe that they merely wanted us to talk to only those people that they represented and not any others who may have learned of our investment interests. Yet, while we there their motivations were not clear at all.

Even with the difficulties, we were introduced to a Christian Chinese couple who are very interested in starting a kindergarten which specializes in English instruction to the children. After listening to their desires and hearing of their commitment to the Lord, we began to discuss in earnest how we could help. When we were finished, we had a plan and we are all praying that we will be able to provide the financial support necessary for them to realize that dream. After all, what better way for our work to be accomplished than by influencing the education of the young ones.

Because of the difficulties which we encountered, we returned to Beijing 3 days early. Upon arriving, it seemed that we had returned to a beautiful clean city compared to where we had been.

These impressions were very strong even though all of us thought that Beijing was one of the dirtiest places we had ever seen only a few short days before. Two more fruitful days passed and I left to return home. Never have I felt the same kind of relief on any other journey as I felt when finally getting on that 747 going to Tokyo.

China does leave many lasting impressions First, it is my opinion that the opening of the barriers to Western business has started a ball rolling which will grow like a snowball. This communist country has started an inevitable movement toward more world involvement and integration into the world community. I don't know if it will collapse like the USSR but I am certain that we will see change of much greater magnitude within a very few years. Missionary work now done under covert means will be able to proceed under much more favorable circumstances. It may not recognize religious freedoms quickly, but it will happen long before that government thinks. The people embrace everything foreign and have begun vast education programs to learn the universal English language.

It's a country of contrasts. Inside the very Western hotels, everything is as nice as one could expect. However, that stops 10 feet outside the front door for there you enter a very different world of undeveloped impoverished people. It's a country of facades. Modern phones are in hotel rooms but don't work properly. Hotels are modern but there is a sign in the bathroom that says the water is not fit to drink. Behind a pretty clean wall is a filthy muddy mess. Yes, the first impressions of China are very lasting. — Roger Reese

MA

The home where we are in Northern China is a simple four room apartment on the sixth floor (no elevator) of a nine-floor apartment building. There are about one hundred apartments in the building, and it is situated in the midst of twenty to thirty other buildings just like it. Go about 1/2 mile and you will find another complex just like this one; in fact, there are hundreds of apartment complexes like this in the city of eight million people.

From my window I can count scores of such apartment buildings. Each of the newer complexes has a central park with newly planted grass and trees, tiled walks lined with benches, and areas to dance and play--with an indoor swimming pool underground, an oasis in the midst of a concrete maze. There are many other older parks that serve certain areas of the city.

At daybreak a few people seem to wander into the park and eventually, within an hour, hundreds of people are milling about. Some bring their songbirds in the bamboo cages, lift the cover from the cage and set the cage on the grass. Twenty to thirty birds begin singing, and the owners (mostly older men) sit around discussing whatever old Chinese men discuss. The birds chatter among themselves whatever birds chatter. Others (men and women) gather in groups and with large fans go through their Tai Chi exercises for an hour. Later, they swap their large, red fans for cheap ornamental swords and practice graceful, chorused movements. Some walk the perimeter of the park in exercise fashion, swinging their arms, too busy for much talk. Much older folk merely saunter along, hands clasped behind their back, and enjoy the cool mornng breeze.
(Sue joins in with Chinese Tai Qui)

As Sue and I wander around the park, several people stop us to ask where are we from, how do we like China, why are we there, etc. All of them afford excellent opportunities for us to practice our little Chinese and them, their little English. People offer us their little canvas chairs or seats on the bench, wiped dry from the morning dew. Hospitality to foreigners--especially Americans--is unbelievable. In the Philippines, where much Filipino and American blood mingle together in the soil from WW II, memories are short. There is some degree of hospitality in the Philippines, moreso in the rural areas than the cities like Manila, Davao, and General Santos but nothing compares to China. More importantly, all such casual meetings give an open door to begin relationships. Each morning brings you back to friends met the day before, and new ones.

One Chinese man who talked with me was a retired English teacher and had interesting opinions as to the advantages of capitalism over socialism. He was very outspoken that individual liberty was much to be preferred over what China offered. I never introduce politics into conversation and attempt to avoid discussion of it by all means. We are not here to educate people on politics or make any political statement. Our interest is strictly spiritual. People need to be saved. Although his foreign travel had only been to Hong Kong and Manila Philippines, he saw enough in those places to educate him on freedom and liberty. I moved the subject of conversation as soon as possible. What a wonderful thing it would be to develop a friendly relationship so that I can ask him if he has ever heard of Jesus and what he thinks of Him. But these matters are not handled in a buttonhole manner in China. Relationships must be developed due to culture and dangers to both your hearer and you. You must know *who* you are witnessing to in China. More than one missionary has faced "unfortunate problems" in renewing visas.

Another problem is a cultural one. Chinese have more than one "yes." A "yes" may mean, "I acknowledge that you said something but I don't think you know anything at all." Of course free-wheeling, charismatic, glory seekers on a religious two-week tour to win all of China, think the jubilant smiles and nods to their religious talk mean, "We have totally agreed to everything you have said." Brag sheets back home print the amazing experience of Pentecost re-experienced and more money hits the coffers to fund another useless expedition.

As the sun rises and heats the day, many leave for work; the park loses the vigorous activity by mid-morning. Only a handful come and go during the remaining sun-bathed hours. Sweepers enter the park and clean up a surprisingly small amount of paper or trash.

Night begins to fall and the park takes on another character--
but still a friendly, safe, and social gathering place. The
neighborhood street dance begins with all ages taking part. Red
flags are waved in unison as the dancers begin an effortless, two
step shuffle in a line of twos, to the blare of live Chinese horns and
drums, playing traditional tunes. This goes on for about thirty
minutes. At the same time, two separate groups gather in large,
tiled, floor areas. One group is made up of beginners; the other are
the more experienced. They dance to waltzes, polkas, and simple
two step, slow tunes played over the loudspeakers. It is not
unusual to hear *The Tennessee Waltz*, *Auld Lang Syne*, *Unchained
Melody,* or some piece from *The Sound of Music*. Only married men
and women dance together, and here and there, two older widows
dance together. Sometimes a person dances alone. No rock music--
no rap--no sensual movements--just folks having a good time.
Younger children rollerblade in an area and others simply play and
run. At 8:30pm the music stops, the lights go out, and people
gradually melt away, leaving the park for a few young lovers to sit
on the benches.

Yuan Su Zhen is 74. Often, she looks out her window
at all the people in the park below. Her back is bent and her joints
are swollen with arthritus. She, like many older Chinese, never
learned to dance. Life was not easy in her former years. Her feet
were bound when she was a baby to keep them from being large
and ugly. Small feet on a Chinese woman in those days were more
desirable than a face and figure like Marilyn Monroe.

Her memory is filled with both joy and sorrow.

She remembers well the Red Guard and the Cultural Revolution of the early, unorganized ruffians loosed on China to eliminate educated and wealthy Chinese, and anyone else who was a threat to Chairman Mao in the early Seventies. She remembers the surrender and melting of home cooking pots and utensils for the communal kitchens and the cause of Communism. Her grandfather was a Christian but she refused his witness of Christ to her. Sometimes she goes out for a walk, or to buy vegetables at the street market, but it is painful and for the most part, she stays inside. Su Zhen is affectionally known as "Ma" and is the mother of our Chinese friend with whom we stay.

My wife, Sue, struck up a good relationship with Ma, a friendship that has extended over five years. Sue always brings her a special gift, looks out for her, and gives her those hugs an older person longs for. Last evening, friendship and a consistent witness of the grace of God, brought eternal benefits; Ma accepted Jesus Christ as her Saviour. After some casual conversation about God, sin, and death, Ma said, "I believe. I accept Jesus." It was so simple. No argument. No more talk. Ma had said before that she tried to do good things--and she did. But now she knows that Jesus is the only one with whom God is pleased.

The reason I mention "Ma" is that it just struck me in a strange way, how that for the most part, USA Christianity is caught up with one of two extremes. One extreme is almost total capitulation; we are so ritualistic to attend 11AM services and insist on an inoffensive "talk" and do nothing aggressive, "love" our neighbor--and know no Bible.

The other extreme is that we minutely examine doctrine to the "nth" degree--arguing over some denominational specialty, raging at KJV versus all else, John's baptism, post, pre, split factions, anabaptists vs baptists, local vs universal church, ripping and tearing, and devouring anybody who dares to differ. But both extremes, for the most part, care nothing for others while they carry on their holy interests. Lost souls all around us seem to be a last priority.

Meanwhile, the Ma's of this world live and die and go to hell without anybody caring. It did not take deep Bible knowledge to win Ma. It took love, patience, compassion, and the simple gospel. Ma will never have a complacent pew to occupy or know anything about the 3 missionary journeys of Paul, the difference between post and pre millennialism, Methodists, Catholics, Bereans, or Baptists, or manuscript evidence. I wonder who will be the better off at the Judgment Seat--Ma and simple witnesses who win people like her, or the sedated crowd and the doctrinal whiz kids who have all doctrines in neat packages but hardly ever win one soul to Christ?

This is not an argument against Bible study, correct doctrine, or church attendance. But it just strikes me as odd that we have appropriated Bible truth to these ends. There should be an overwhelming desire to put all these doctrinal creeds into a pair of shoes that goes to the Ma's and others like her, not to make them one of us, but to bring them to Christ. –Dave and Sue Reese

FUNERAL IN MAINLAND CHINA

We went to the old four floor apartment building. It was winter weather, 20 degrees and in NE China. 25-30 people were standing in the bitter cold outside. There were various colored wreaths of paper on several individuals. Close relatives (other than the wife) such as the son and daughter, wore white cloth draped over their heads and tied at waist. Others wore colored arm bands of black. The daughter carried her father's picture, an 8" X 10" framed and edged with black crepe paper.

Sue and I stood in the small bedroom with the wife for a few minutes. There were no chairs except one on which she sat. We went back down 3 floors to a car which drove to the hospital.

The body was in the hospital's metal storage shed—12 compartments in a makeshift morgue, 20' X 30'. Six men (pallbearers) pulled on white gloves and took the body from the cold storage slab. The corpse was covered with a yellow cloth. The son took a cluster of cotton and touched the head: to indicate the family accepted his death; then the hands: indicating he would have money for his travel to the unseen world; then feet to have a peaceful and easy journey. His wife and daughter were held up bodily by the relatives to see the deceased amid much wailing and fainting.

Then the body was placed into a waiting vehicle, a type of hearse, for the trip to the crematorium. Before the hearse left, the son and daughter and other relatives bowed on their knees before a stone pot about 14" to 18" in diameter and lit the paper in it (so he could have money on his journey). The son raised the pot above his head and slammed it to the ground shatttering it in pieces and yelled, "zai jian baba!!!" (Goodbye father!!) There were more crying and loud wailing as all got into cars and drove to crematorium.

The crematorium was composed of four large buildings about 15 miles from the hospital. The street leading up to it was lined with people selling gold and silver paper boxes-plus many other types of hell bank notes along with some wreaths. *(Hell bank notes are paper imitations of various money denominations. "Hell' in Chinese culture is the unseen world where dead people have living accommodations. By burning literal paper imitations of money, clothes, car, etc., the items are spiritually transferred from earth to hell.)* We all stood outside on the porch until a man yelled (literally) for us to come in. All moved in a counterclockwise motion the around the body which laid in a U shaped flower area on a wheeled gurney. The man's picture was projected on a wall screen. The man had a hat and sandals and was covered with yellow cloth. His full name and occupation was also projected in a computer ribbon display. All the mourners walked around and bowed with their heads toward the body.

The attendant yelled "bow three times to your father!" — then he said "Leave!". The wall computerized picture changed to an old lady, who was next "service". The whole *service* took about ten minutes. The body was wheeled out before we were out of the room and the old lady wheeled in for the next. This goes on all day from 8 AM to 6 PM, every day, 7 days every week.

We then went to an adjacent building where you pay for services, select an urn, and wait on the ashes. It took 30 minutes.

Hottest furnace for crematory cost 500 yuan (about $60 USD), the next is 220, the next is 120 yuan. Then separate charges for things like an engraved name on the ash box---4 yuan per letter. This is how 1 body is disposed of every 3 seconds in Atheistic China. ----Dave and Sue Reese

DAVE'S CONVERSION

The black 1955 Chevy roared down the dirt road with a Tennessee State Trooper in close pursuit. As the road behind the Chevy turned into an impenetrable cloud of blinding dust, the high school teens laughed and passed around the bootleg gin they had just bought. The redhead in the front passenger seat felt the exhilaration of the close brush with the law. A month later he stood on a roadside picnic table and splattered a watermelon on a passing State Trooper car. One of his friends was caught but he and the others eluded the police by running through the woods to a side road where their car was parked.

Although he was almost killed in a car wreck in April of 1955, it did not stop his wild career. After an eighteen inch steel pin was placed in his leg, he contracted a deadly infection, osteomyelitis, but miraculously survived. The six weeks in the hospital and confining months spent in a wheelchair and on crutches did not slow him down. After high school graduation, the school building was set on fire. The redhead was a suspect. Although he had nothing to do with the fire, his reputation was already set.

When his best friend enrolled at Memphis State University, Dave enrolled at The Memphis Academy of Arts, determined to become a commercial artist. However, the night life and wild times of the past continued in Memphis. It was the beginning of rock n' roll and Sun Record Company in Memphis. It wasn't long until Dave had met all the budding stars at Sun. He became friends with a record store owner's son. Through that friendship he met Elvis, Jerry Lee Lewis, Roy Orbison, Johnny Cash, Carl Perkins plus a few other hopefuls that never reached their status. It wasn't long until he had a guitar and struggled to learn the chords, aspiring to become a recording artist.

He was almost shot one night by a security guard at a resort he and his friend planned to rob. After two years in Memphis and several more close involvement's with the police, Dave left Memphis and his friends. The music plans didn't work out. Out of boredom more than anything else, he joined the USAF. Basic training was completed in San Antonio, Texas and he was assigned Technical school at Scott AFB, Illinois. When he was off duty, loneliness drove him to the nightclubs of Belleville and St. Louis.

One night in a Belleville restaurant, his gaze stopped on a girl that was strangely different from the others. She was 5'8", slim, and wore a black dress. Four months later, on Easter morning, Dave asked Sue to marry him. "I can't cook", she answered. "That's all right. My mom will teach you." She went to church that morning and Dave went back to duty at Scott field.

When orders came for Dave to report to Langley AFB, Virginia, he left, promising they would get together soon. However, he really didn't know what to do. The responsibility of marriage scared him one moment and the stability of being with Sue appealed to him at another. In fact, when Sue went to church services, Dave regularly dated a Catholic girl he had also met in Belleville. He did not want to go to church. The Protestant girl went to church on Sunday evening as well as morning, but the Catholic girl didn't go on Sunday night. At the time, it seemed to be an excellent arrangement as far as he was concerned! In Virginia, it didn't take long for the loneliness, music, and old nature to drive him back to the bars. This time it was Buckroe and Virginia beaches and another girl.

He tried to forget Sue back in Illinois but found it more difficult than he imagined. He couldn't get her out of his mind. One day he wrote her and said if she wanted to marry him, she had better come to Virginia right away. Otherwise, it was all off. To Dave's surprise, she arrived on a bus within a few days.

Marriage didn't slow down his love of music. When he received orders for assignment on a remote radar site in Bethel, Alaska he had become proficient enough to
entertain others by singing and playing the guitar. Once in Alaska he played and sang at the base officer's club. Invited to enter a USO show troop in 1959, he almost joined but decided to go home to his wife and two children.

Once home, music led him on a wild, ungodly path that almost cost him his marriage and family. His wife, Sue, had been saved as a teenager and knew the nightclub life was wrong. She prayed for Dave and took their two children, Cindy and Sandra, to church each Sunday.

One Saturday evening in 1963 Dave's world changed. While singing a country song (*"Please Release Me"*) at the American Legion Hall in Centerville Alabama, he was struck with the thought: "This is a dead end street!". Cigarette smoke hung over the dancing couples like a fog—but Dave realized very clearly that he was on the way to Hell.

Arriving home that night about midnight, he told Sue, "I've got to get my life straightened out. What can I do?" Sue simply answered: "You need to trust Jesus." Thinking the only place you could do that was at the foot of their bed (where Sue knelt every night to pray) he bowed at the foot of the bed and asked Jesus to save him.

No angels appeared, no lights flashed, but when he arose he felt as though a heavy burden had been lifted off his back. The next morning, he led his wife and daughters to church. He has been there ever since!

A 98 CENT BIBLE

Shopping for Christmas presents in 1962, we approached the checkout line. My eyes caught sight of a barrel of Bibles on sale for 98 cents. I wanted one, but we didn't have much money. My only Bible was in a teacher's desk in Illinois, 600 miles from Selma, Alabama. We added the little white Holy Bible to our purchases and headed home.

That evening I gathered Cindy and Sandra to my side and said, "Mama wants to read you a story." I began with Luke's account of Jesus' birth. It became a regular practice for me to gather my girls to me at evening time and read to them God's Word. Somehow my husband always got busy and had "something" to do in another part of the house during this time.

One evening after we were all in bed, I cautiously asked Dave to kneel and pray with me. We never had before. He did so. We prayed. He called upon Jesus to forgive and save him. Later, as he recounted that time, he said it was the word of God that convicted him of how sinful his life was, and that without Christ, he surely would have died and gone to hell. Reading a Bible verse really convicted him.

From that time on, Dave was indeed a new creature in Christ (II Corinthians 5:17). Shortly after his conversion, he was called to preach. Today, as I sit and listen to him preach I am so thankful for the blessed word of God. It changed our entire home and life together. The word of God united us truly as one in Christ. Because of a 98 cent King James Bible, my husband will be with me forever in heaven. ---Sue Reese

"For the word of God is quick, and powerful, and sharper than any twoedged sword, piercing even to the dividing asunder of soul and spirit, and of the joints and marrow, and is a discerner of the thoughts and intents of the heart." Hebrews 4:12.

SUE'S TESTIMONY

"For after that in the wisdom of God the world by wisdom knew not God, it pleased God by the foolishness of preaching to save them that believe." (1 Corinthians 1:21 KJB)

I attended a small church when I was 8 years old. Some of my aunts and cousins attended before my mother and grandmother died. It was the only Baptist church in the town.

I enjoyed singing and attending Bible school and the Sunday School classes. Sometime after my mother died, a faithful Sunday School teacher took me to a revival at a Baptist church in a neighboring town.

The preacher preached on Hell and told all about it as if he had seen it. He made it a terrible place and I believed it was. So when he gave an invitation to accept Jesus Christ who died on the cross to pay for all our sins, past, present, and future, I was ready to take this Saviour as mine.

They carefully dealt with me because I was only 8 years old. They questioned me and my answer was "Yes. I believe Jesus died for me!"

All these years have passed since I was 8 years old but Jesus has been all the Bible says He is. He is my Friend; He is my Comforter; He is my Help. He has never failed to guide my steps. When I've strayed, it is me that was wrong, not Jesus.

I asked Him to give me a good husband, He did. I asked Him to give me children, He did. All my children are saved. I am not afraid of the future because I know the Lord will show me the way. I am not afraid of death because when I close my eyes in death, I will awake in the house of my Friend, my Saviour, my Lord.

If you do not know Jesus, seek to know Him. If you know Him, follow Him. Eternity is forecer! Where you spend it is your decision. Death will seal that decision—Heaven or Hell. What do you choose? – Sue Reese